British SPECIALIST CARS

ATLANTIS

British SPECIALIST CARS

Chris Rees

Postwar Low-volume Production Cars and Kit Cars

Windrow & Greene Automotive

Published in Great Britain by
Windrow & Greene Ltd
5 Gerrard Street
London W1V 7LJ

A C.I.P. catalogue record for this book is available from the British Library.

ISBN 1 872004 22 9

Designed by:
ghk DESIGN, Chiswick, London

Advertising Sales:
Boland Advertising & Publishing

Printed by
Craft Print (Europe) Ltd

FRONT COVER ILLUSTRATIONS
Top Left: *Dax Rush*
Top right: *Elva Courier*
Centre: *Ginetta G33*
Bottom: *Hudson Free Spirit*

BACK COVER ILLUSTRATIONS
Top: *NG TF*
Bottom: *Marlin Berlinetta*

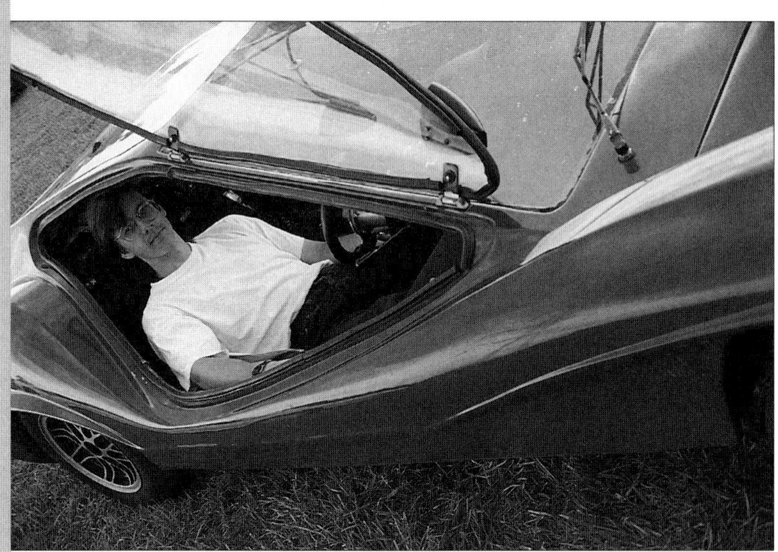

The Author

Judging by his obsession with the subject, **Chris Rees'** interest in cars must have begun in the womb. His first spoken word was 'Mini'.

Chris began working for *Kit Car* magazine over ten years ago and joined the staff of *Alternative Cars* in 1983. After a spell not making any money in the music business, he devoted himself full-time to not making any money in freelance journalism, contributing regularly to *Classic & Sportscar*, *Autocar & Motor*, *Your Classic*, *World Sportscars* and a variety of kit car magazines.

Aged 29, he lives in Berkshire with his wife, Gabriella, and three children, plus an assortment of bizarre vehicles including a Centaur kit car and a three-wheeled Citroen 2CV.

This book is dedicated to Gabriella.

CONTENTS

***Above:** Since 1989 Caterham Cars have offered a replica of the Lotus Seven featured, and shown here, in the 1967 cult television series,* The Prisoner.

ACKNOWLEDGEMENTS

Many thanks to everyone who has helped with this book and in particular to the following:

Gary Axon, for the almost unfathomable depths of his knowledge;

Peter Filby, of *Which Kit?* magazine, whose efforts over the years have generated enormous interest in the subject and who supplied many of the pictures;

Ian Hyne, of *Kitcars International* magazine, for his support and for the supply of numerous pictures;

Darren Styles and the Ford Sidevalve Owners Club, for the use of a number of photographs.

INTRODUCTION

The world of specialist cars is one of the richest, most diverse and most baffling planets in motoring cosmology. Contained within it are the fruits of an unending labour of love whose sole end is to create something different. From the excruciating to the extraordinary, the derisory to the sublime, you could hardly find a more expansive cross-section of cars.

At the bottom end are amateur engineers building one-offs and offering kits of parts, or even sets of plans, for other DIY mechanics to build their own examples. At the top are some of the most expensive, exclusive and opulent cars ever made. In between is a bewildering array of sports cars, fun cars, grand tourers, jeeps, beach buggies, supercars, three-wheelers, six-wheelers, eight-wheelers, off-roaders, road-going racers, replicas, exotics, microcars, electric cars, steam cars and limousines.

The one thing holding this tremendous variety of specialist cars together is that they all provide an alternative to a mainstream which has become increasingly boring and predictable. Specialist cars aim (albeit with varying degrees of success) to put excitement back into motoring, to offer an exclusive means of transport and to provide ideas, styles and driving pleasure never approached in the research departments of Rover, Vauxhall, Ford or VW.

In Britain the specialist car has become something of an institution. There has been no shortage of willing enthusiasts prepared to invest the energy required to build and manufacture their own visions of the ideal car. Helped by laws which are kind to small-time constructors, many a new design — often of real worth — has been cobbled up in a garage after normal working hours.

And there has always been a healthy demand for the offbeat. Building your own car has the twin advantages of low price and satisfaction. At the opposite end, Britain's specialist sports and luxury car makers have traditionally attracted a loyal following of enthusiasts fascinated by these hand-built cars.

This book aims to fill a gaping void. Why no-one has yet attempted to write a book on the subject of the specialist marques of Britain becomes apparent after even the most cursory amount of research: it is an historian's nightmare, a singular morass of convoluted tales, obscurity and incestuousness. Unravelling it all is like tackling a plate of Gordian spaghetti. Conflicting accounts, sparse documentation and the failing memories of the people involved in making the cars all contribute to a near-impossible task.

So what is a specialist car? For the purposes of this book, I have limited the contents to all low-volume road cars produced, or intended for production, in

Britain since 1945. Broadly speaking, these split into two categories: kit cars and fully-built, or coachbuilt, cars.

There is no precise definition of what is meant by 'low-volume'. Probably the highest-volume car in the book is the Bond Bug, over 2,500 of which were made, although some kit car firms claim to have sold more than this. But you won't find the larger so-called specialists here, firstly because they are not low-volume in the sense of most of the marques covered in this book and, secondly, because they are very adequately dealt with in other books devoted to individual marques. A central reason for writing this book is that it documents cars which have never been covered anywhere else.

So you won't read here about Reliant, Rolls-Royce or Lotus. Only a few off-beat creations of these larger fringe manufacturers get a mention: peripheral Aston Martins and TVRs, for instance.

Quite a few entries can be found for 'manufacturers' who only ever built one car. These get in because there was a serious intention to put the car into production. Strict one-offs are excluded, as are models where there was only the vaguest scheme to enter production — probably hatched over a pint in a pub and forgotten about the next morning.

Likewise, modified versions of mainstream production cars are excluded. Between Ford Escorts with spoilers on and an all-new chassis and body which happens to use a Ford Escort engine, a line must be drawn somewhere. It is often a rather vague line, but generally you won't find entries for cars which are not substantially original.

That eliminates conversion specialists like Crayford, bodykit purveyors like Cartel, go-faster modifiers like Tickford and Superspeed and body alterers like Harrington. Drawing the line on the last category is sometimes quite difficult: for example, I have excluded the Broadspeed Mini, whose front half and floorpan was basically a Mini; but I have included the Sherwood, which used a Ford Cortina centre body section.

All models must have been intended for road use. Therefore pure race cars and off-road 'rails' are out, but dual-purpose cars are in. Street and hot rods, many of which were sold in kit form in the UK, are excluded. Some microcars also get a mention, but that subject really deserves a book of its own.

As for the 'Made in Britain' requirement, I have kept out cars which were made abroad and imported by British companies to be sold here. But foreign designs which were manufactured in Britain do get in. And there are some borderline cases. For instance, Radbourne built several Abarths in this country but used Italian bodyshells on new Simca 1000 floorpans from France. That one didn't make it in.

Finally, I have included an A-Z of British Specialist Cars at the rear of the book which attempts to list comprehensively all the low-volume cars made in Britain since the war. I say 'attempts' because I long ago gave up the idea that such a directory could ever be one hundred percent complete. Undoubtedly I have left off some obscure moorland manufacturer, and new discoveries (as my editor will confirm) keep cropping up all the time. Anyone who recognises any omission or inaccuracy in the book is welcome to get in touch with me via the publisher.

This book is dedicated to all car enthusiasts, to those who delight in the obscure, and to the creative spirit of invention.

PART ONE

Postwar British Specialist Cars

Mantara — a new chapter in the Marcos story

Stranger than fiction. In 1965, as described on page 13, Jim Parkinson drove his 1935 Rytecraft Scootacar all the way round the world.

Chapter One

The Early Days – when all Manufacturers were Specialists

Every motor car manufacturer of the earliest years was a specialist. Before the arrival of mass production, there was no such thing as a 'mainstream': firms generally cobbled together their horseless carriages from the absolute basics up. Taking components from related industries, almost any engineer could construct a viable motor car. It was even common to create one's own internal combustion (or indeed steam or electric) engine from scratch.

Experiment was the norm, and there were certainly some novel ideas in evidence. Amazingly, the first attempt at a two-wheeled gyroscopically controlled car came in 1900, with the Lawson gyrocar. Even Wolseley tried the idea successfully in 1913. Then there were cars with six, and even eight, wheels. The Reeves Octo-Auto used four axles in an effort to improve ride quality and, in 1902, Sunbeam tried four wheels arranged in a diamond pattern.

As the design and manufacturing standards of cars took their first steps towards uniformity, 'specialist' branches of the industry began to form. These ranged from the ultra-basic cyclecar to the full coachbuilt limousine constructed to order on contemporary chassis. Already, distinctions were being made between the emerging mainstream and what the smaller manufacturer could offer.

In the case of cyclecars, which emerged as an identifiable breed around 1910, this took the form of a very cheap and very simple design which just about anyone could run. Cyclecars enjoyed increasing popularity until, in the 1920s, some of the bigger firms saw the potential of the mass-market and produced their own cheaper cars: Ford's Model T is the shining example, having marked out the path as early as 1908. In Britain, the Austin Seven (1922) effectively brought the cyclecar era to an end by offering big car sophistication in miniature.

Those early cyclecars were true alternatives and sired such long-lived gems as the Morgan Super Sports three-wheeler (made until 1952) and, ultimately, the bubble car.

It was the cyclecars which were probably the first true kit cars ever made. During the height of the boom, many firms prospered selling parts only, which DIY enthusiasts could build up into complete cars — the object being to keep down costs, of course. This was a procedure not adopted again until the 1950s and the emergence of the glassfibre bodyshell industry.

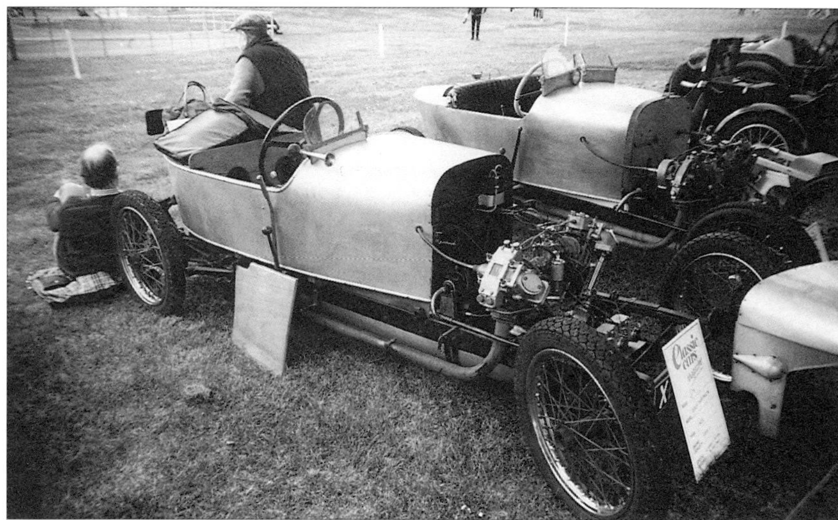

Left: *One of the best and most popular cyclecars was the GN, a spindly little sporting machine which brought motoring to the masses.*

GN

The GN was the archetypal British cyclecar and one of the most popular of the breed. Combining simplicity with very low prices, the GN might justly be described as the first practical 'car for the masses', production having started at Hendon, Middlesex, in 1911.

The cars were extremely light (only 6.5cwt) and were consequently attractive to competition-minded customers. The GN and other cars like it were often used as the basis of 'specials' constructed by amateurs on parts supplied by serious manufacturers. By 1925, however, like most of its kind, the GN had died.

Austin Seven Specials

The car which killed the cyclecar in Britain was the Austin Seven. Equally cheap to buy, it offered the design characteristics of larger cars in a very compact package. It was 'popular' cars such as the Seven which largely ousted smaller manufacturers from their position as suppliers of cars for mainstream customers, forcing them to offer specialised models — or to go out of business altogether.

This could be said to be the origin of the specialist car business as it is known today: small firms occupying 'market niches' of proven, but low-volume, sales. Traditionally, it is an area where the larger manufacturers are by their very nature reluctant to tread.

Many individuals built specials on popular cars: the separate chassis of pre-war cars allowed for the fitment of completely new bodywork with as sophisticated a design as the builder could manage. The Model T Ford, pre-war Ford 10 and Morris Eight were popular choices for the specials builders.

But it was probably ageing Austin Sevens, which could be bought as bangers for next to nothing, which provided the amateur enthusiast with the easiest opportunity to make an interesting car for himself. The trend was consolidated in the 1950s, with the arrival of glassfibre as a material for car bodywork.

Firms also offered steel bodywork to replace ageing and rusty Seven shells. (The example pictured in this chapter is in fact a modern replica of the Gordon Cup Seven, using original Austin Seven chassis and mechanicals.) This provided Seven owners with the means to prolong the life of their cars — one of the essential *raisons d'être* of the specialist car industry.

Rytecraft Scootacar

The Rytecraft Scootacar could be described as a joke which became a reality. Developed from a fairground dodgem car, it at first used almost exclusively in funfairs. But somehow, from 1934, it made it on to the road and remained available for seven years.

The road must have been a distinctly uncomfortable place for this 98cc-engined 'car'. With a top speed of just 15mph, it was impressive chiefly for the items it lacked: springs, gears, brake pedal, lights, windscreen, bumpers and mudguards. Luckily, the design mellowed with age, gaining a reverse gear, lights and two seats, still at a cost of only £80.

By the time the Scootacar ceased production in 1940, an amazing 1,500 examples had been sold. It seemed to hold an immense appeal for celebrities and eccentrics, attracting custom from owners with bizarre tastes to states with bizarre owners, such as King Zog of Albania.

The Scootacar enjoyed a revival in 1965, when enthusiast Jim Parkinson hit upon the adventurous notion of driving one round the world. Having rebuilt his 1935 car, he tested it for just one hour before embarking. He left via Dover and drove through Europe to Moscow where the authorities, doubting his sanity, refused to let him continue his planned route across Russia and forced him to travel on the Trans-Siberian railway to Vladivostock.

At his next port of call, Japan, he was treated as a hero, before boarding a ship to San Francisco and driving the 3,000 miles to New York. His return to Britain occurred just 421 days after his departure, surely one of the bravest trans-global expeditions ever accomplished.

English Mechanic

Perhaps the first-ever build-it-yourself car was the English Mechanic. No factory selling cars or even parts ever existed: instead, in January 1900, the magazine *The English Mechanic and World of Science and Art* launched a weekly series of articles on how to build your own small car.

Several designs were mooted, including petrol- and steam-powered three- and four-wheelers. The last articles appeared in July 1905, after which the magazine turned its attention to build-it-yourself pianolas. At least two English Mechanics are known to survive.

Below: *This fabric-bodied Gordon Cup Special is a modern replica based on the car which killed most early specialists — the Austin Seven.*

Above: *The world's first kit car? All English Mechanics were built from plans published in a science magazine from 1900 to 1905.*

Left: *Morris made one of the first multi-wheelers, this 6D six-wheeler, based on a 6x4 army command car, in 1930-31. Only about 20 were made.*

Chapter Two

Specials and Bubbles of the 1950s

The years immediately following the war were particularly barren for the specialist car. Austerity measures, supply difficulties and a stringent government policy of 'export or die' meant that motoring was available only to the privileged few. The notion of private sports cars was far from most people's minds, or means.

But as the worst of the shortages eased and petrol became more freely available, a new era of popular motoring began. Two factors helped the birth of a completely new type of vehicle: the kit car. These were, firstly, the availability of cheap bangers with separate chassis and, secondly, the dissemination of a new wonder-material, glassfibre.

Glassfibre reinforced plastic (GRP) effectively brought about an explosion of amateur car makers. In raw matt form it was cheap to buy and could readily be shaped into the sort of curves which would take a skilled coachbuilder hours to form in metal each time. By simply making a mould, any number of bodyshells or panels could be made without labour-intensive methods. The only reason glassfibre was not adopted for mass-production cars was the time it took for each shell to cure in its mould; thus, for large runs, an uneconomic number of moulds would be required. However, GRP was perfect for the small manufacturer.

In the days of separate chassis ('monocoque' was a very new term in the 1950s), it was a simple matter to create any type of body you wished on a contemporary chassis. Because of its popularity and cheapness, most designers opted for the Ford Ten/Anglia/Popular chassis with its basic sidevalve engine, or the Austin Seven. Translate your bodywork ideas into GRP and slap it on the chassis, and you were in business.

The first of these cars — which came to be known generically as specials — appeared in the early 1950s and were generally sold as basic bodyshells, leaving all the construction (and often quite a bit of extra manufacture) to be done by the builder. If you bought a good one, you might also get items like doors, headlamps and weather equipment.

These were very basic machines. Some consisted solely of two halves of a body which were intended to fit a variety of chassis and wheelbases, so the constructor had to fabricate bits of the body himself. Not surprisingly, performance from the archaic engines invariably fitted was pitiful.

Yet, as a breed, specials succeeded dramatically. The reason was that there were no other cheap sports cars around in the 1950s — not, at any rate, until the Austin-Healey Sprite of 1958. Many bodyshells looked very attractive and the thought of being able to drive a sports-bodied car for a small outlay was to many enthusiasts irresistible. Sales soared, reaching a heady peak in the years 1958-62 when thousands upon thousands were sold. EB, for instance, claimed to have sold 450 shells within ten months during 1960.

Some firms went one better and offered their own chassis, or used proprietary chassis like the spaceframes from Buckler. With tuned engines, these could become respectable sports cars at last. A few even ventured into aluminium alloy as a material for bodies; others dabbled with monocoques.

But the combined influence of cheaper mass-produced sports cars which could run rings around the antiquated Ford chassis specials, and the halving of purchase tax on fully-built cars, squashed the specials boom flat. Overnight, the existence of the shell makers fluttered out. Shrewd firms like Ginetta and Rochdale moved up-market. Others, like Ashley, diversified into glassfibre panels, hardtops and dinghies. The others became history.

At the same time, there emerged another gateway into austerity motoring: the microcar, or bubble car. This was another peculiarly 1950s phenomenon which attracted all sorts of engineers with curious ideas on how to make a car from the very minimum of materials. Again, the popularity of these tiny conveyances — the smallest the world has ever seen — sustained the breed well into the 1960s.

The typical formula for a 1950s microcar was: three wheels (to take advantage of the UK's tax and licensing laws), a tiny engine (usually no more than 300cc), and the absolute basic specification.

In Britain, Lawrie Bond was the most prolific microcar designer, creating a string of practical three-wheelers under his own name, as well as a few freelance designs for other firms. Unique among the micro-builders of the 1950s, Bond as a marque survived into the 1970s.

Just like the specials, microcars died a sudden death in the early 1960s. The reason was nearly identical: mass-produced cars suddenly got a lot better and a lot cheaper. Interviewed about his design of the Mini, Alec Issigonis stated that it was his loathing for bubble cars which inspired him to create his small family car. Launched in 1959, the Mini burst the bubble car boom almost single-handedly.

Apart from a handful of minor but high-quality marques, such as HRG and Peerless, the 1950s were otherwise devoid of any really significant specialist development. People had to wait until the more prosperous 1960s for real alternatives to emerge.

Right: *1955 Turner A30 Sports: Jack Turner's first attempt at a cheap sports car, based on Austin A30 parts.*

Below: *1961 Turner GT: a pretty fixed-head coupé which was never properly marketed. It is the rarest production Turner.*

Turner

Jack H. Turner made several specials, as well as designing engines, before turning to car manufacture, in which he was one of the more successful and respected specialists of the 1950s. His first cars (1951-52) were real specials, offered as twin-tube chassis with independent transverse springing. Engines were to the choice of the customer, as were bodies, which split into stark cycle-winged bullets and small enclosed bodies. Just seven of these early sports cars were made.

The A30 Sports of 1955 was a more serious enterprise, with a GRP body on Turner's own ladder chassis into which Austin A30 engine, gearbox, brakes and front suspension were fitted: rather like the later Austin-Healey Sprite, in fact. 90 were made before the 950 Sports replaced it in 1957, using A35 engines in the same chassis and a revised body with tiny fins. 170 were built, including some with the alloy Coventry-Climax engine.

Turner's definitive Sports was launched in 1959 with a new body restyled front and rear, still on the same chassis. Coventry-Climax-engined Turners, good for 100mph, scored some competition wins and helped sell 160 cars. The MkII (1960) and MkIII (1963) brought Ford engines to the marque, as well as Triumph Herald front suspension. 150 and 90 of each were sold respectively.

The Turner GT was the only fixed-head Turner, launched in 1961. Styled by Jack Turner, it used an all-new chassis with a monocoque centre section and Cortina 1.5 power (again the Climax engine was optional). The GT was only ever a special-order car and just 9 were sold by 1966, when Jack Turner's illness effectively brought the firm's trading to an end.

Above: *1954 Swallow Doretti: attractive and convincing sports car with TR2 mechanicals. Most went to America.*

Above: *Hardly the most appealing shape of the 1950s specials boom, the Microplas Stiletto was one of the first.*

Below: *The Watford Cheetah was typical of the glassfibre bodies offered by dozens of operators for sidevalve Fords.*

Swallow

Swallow Coachbuilding had its origins in the pre-war firm, SS, which later became Jaguar. Swallow was the sidecar part of the firm, sold off after the war. To compensate for declining sidecar sales, it launched its own sports car, the Swallow Doretti, in 1954.

The Doretti used the mechanicals from a Triumph TR2 and was a crust above the TR with its hand-built aluminium body and leather trim; its price, accordingly, was higher than the TR2's by £230. The Triumph parts fitted into Swallow's own tubular frame with an inner skin of steel. The result was a pleasing touring convertible capable of 100mph (slightly less than the TR2) and it sold rather well: 276 were made in its ten-month life. It was killed off after Jaguar itself objected that its former wing might affect its own sales. A 2+2 coupé version, dubbed the Sabre, never reached production, although three were built.

Microplas

Microplas was one of the very first of the specials manufacturers. Based in Mitcham, it essayed two basic shells which shared the same basic profile. The Stiletto was intended for the 6ft 9in Austin Seven chassis, while the Mistral used the 7ft 6in Ford chassis. Neither was a particularly handsome design, though the Mistral probably had the edge with its twin air vents behind the front wheel arches. It also had the distinction of being used as the prototype shell for the Fairthorpe Electron of 1956.

Cheetah

The Watford Cheetah was typical of the myriad special shells produced, often in home garages, by enterprising engineers. From its base (in Watford, naturally enough), the firm's main trade was in tubular chassis for Ford sidevalve engines, offered with independent front suspension. The Cheetah used this chassis with independent suspension all round, making it one of the more sophisticated specials. The firm lasted, like many of its ilk, from around 1959 to 1962.

Tornado

Tornado was one of the largest and most successful of the specials boom firms. Set up in 1957, its first effort was the Typhoon, a phenomenally ugly car styled by founder Bill Woodhouse and Tony Bunce. It was distinguished by its simple build-up and cheap price (£200 in complete form, with chassis).

Tornado's chassis was a simple steel frame with swing axles to the fore and a live coilsprung rear. Two wheelbase lengths, offering two and four seats, were available, both in open and closed varieties. Either Ford E93A or BMC A-series engines could be fitted. There was even the choice of a Sportsbrake model from 1960, a sort of sporting estate which predated the Scimitar GTE by some 8 years. The Typhoon was the firm's most popular model, around 400 being made.

The Thunderbolt of 1960 was an enlarged Typhoon adapted to accept a TR2 engine. It was a disaster to drive and only one was made, despite replicas being offered at £1500 fully-built.

Using another modified Typhoon chassis and body, the Tempest of 1960 was intended to use Ford Anglia 105E engines, although BMC A-series and Herald units were also fitted. Again available in two lengths, with two or four seats, about 15 were made.

Breaking away from the Typhoon theme was the Talisman, completed in 1961. Sporting rather more acceptable lines penned by Colin Hextall, it was a 2+2 GRP coupé based on a ladder chassis with Herald front suspension and steering column and a choice of Ford engines from 55 to 85bhp - the latter tuned by Cosworth, the first time a Cosworth engine had been fitted in a road car. 100mph was claimed with the most powerful unit. Sold in kit form, or fully built for £1300, it was a package which worked well — and sold well. 186 were made by the time Woodhouse's firm got into financial troubles in 1963. Sold on to another firm which was never really interested in production, the marque died in 1964, although an attempt was later made to launch a revised Talisman, unsuccessfully.

Above: *The very first sports estate was the Tornado Typhoon Sportsbrake of 1960, based on the highly successful Typhoon roadster.*

Right: *Tornado's Talisman of 1961 was something of a legend in its day, handsome, fast and a fine handler. But it was rather expensive compared with cars such as the Gilbern.*

Above: *1962 Ashley Sportiva: one of the most popular and professional of the Ford-based specials.*

Ashley

Ashley Laminates was one of the early special shell makers, founded by Keith Waddington and Peter Pellandine in 1954. Its first shell was intended for Austin Seven parts and proved highly successful, 500 being sold during the 1950s. Pellandine very soon left to form Falcon Shells, leaving Waddington to work on a Ford E93A based shell, called the 1172. This was available in open and closed forms for long and short wheelbases. Ashley's own ladder chassis could also be used from 1958, with engines including Ford 105E, BMC and MGA. The hardtop 1172 was generally known as the Ashley GT.

The Sportiva of 1962 was an open headlamp version of the 1172, again available in open and closed and two and four-seat versions. Ashley withdrew its kits with the collapse of the business in 1962 to concentrate on other glassfibre work. An Ashley 1172 was used as the basis of the Sabra/Reliant Sabre of 1961.

Falcon

Falcon was the name Peter Pellandine gave to his company after he split from Ashley in the early 1950s. His first shell, the Mk1, was identical to the Ashley 750 and was intended for Austin Seven parts. The better-looking Ford based Mk2 was the shell used by Elva in its works sports racer. Simple twin-tube chassis were also available from Falcon for the princely sum of £50.

The Caribbean was the firm's most successful model, selling about 2,000 examples by the time it departed in 1963. It was a pretty two-seater for Ford 10 mechanicals, available in open and closed forms. Falcon enlisted the services of Len Terry (of Terrier), who designed the spaceframe chassis which often sat under Caribbean shells, later with independent front suspension. Optionally, other engines, including Coventry-Climax and MGA, could be fitted. In 1961 came the four-seater coupé version of the Caribbean, the Bermuda. Uglier and cramped in the back, it sold only 200 examples.

The earlier Mk2 shell formed the basis of the Competition. This was an attractive two-seater introduced in 1958, initially intended as a cheap means of getting yourself on the track. Its most celebrated version was the open model with twin head fairings, although normal open and hardtop Competitions were also available from just £65 for the bare shell. This was also Pellandine's first genuine complete kit,

Right: *About 2,000 Falcon Caribbeans were made up to 1963, the result of good looks and the availability of a chassis with independent front suspension.*

Below: *Surely the most beautiful shape born of the specials phenomenon was the 1963 Falcon 515 which died before it had a chance to sell in any quantity.*

sold at £560 with the spaceframe chassis for Ford 105E components.

Falcon's next move — an attempt to break into more serious territory — occurred after Peter Pellandine had emigrated to Australia, later to found the Pellandine marque (Chapter Five). The new model was the 515, a highly attractive coupé styled by a Brazilian, Tom Rohonyi. Shown at the 1963 Racing Car Show, it enjoyed favourable reviews. Based on a multi-tubular spaceframe chassis, its GRP body was bonded on and proved strong and well-finished. Most used a twin-carb Cortina 1.5-litre engine, good for 70bhp. Complete kits cost £900 and fully-built cars were also offered, but only 25 515s were built before Falcon wound up in early 1964.

There had been another model, the Falcon 1000 of 1961, which was taken on by an independent company, Peregrine Cars, in the factory vacated by Falcon in 1959. Just two were made.

Berkeley

Lawrie Bond, the prodigious microcar designer, approached Charles Panter of Berkeley Coachworks in 1955 with the idea that he should build his idea for a micro sports car. Previously, Berkeley had pioneered the art of glassfibre as early as 1948 in its caravans. Panter agreed and Bond built three prototypes in 1956. The result was a tiny (10ft 2in) car of GRP unitary construction and independent suspension all round, weighing just 5.5cwt. Even with the tiny 322cc Anzani engine (15bhp), it was a nippy little car. Known as the B60, it was an instant success.

But supply problems with the Anzani led Panter to source another engine, the 328cc Excelsior unit, and the model was renamed the B65. An excellent performer (top speed 65mph), with keen handling and braking, it won significant praise. But Bond's chassis could easily handle more power, so the B90 was launched in 1958 with a 492cc three-cylinder version of the Excelsior unit and a four-speed 'box instead of three speeds. Berkeley's numbering system was based on its models' top speeds: it followed that the B90 could achieve 90mph. Both two- and four-seat versions were offered.

In the search for an engine more suited to its American market, Panter fitted his first four-stroke to a Berkeley, the Royal Enfield 692cc twin in 1959. With two states of tune churning out 40 and 50bhp, the two new models were known as the B95 and B105 respectively. They could be distinguished by their revised nose treatment incorporating a rectangular grille.

Panter decided to modify the rear end of the B65 and create a three-wheeler called the T60, launched in October 1959. It was an instant smash hit, knocking most other micro three-wheelers for six. Using the 328cc Excelsior engine, it notched up an incredible 2,500 sales in just over a year; the four-wheelers had sold 2,000 in total.

By the end of 1960, it was all over for Berkeley. The caravan business had collapsed and dragged the car side with it. Berkeley's potential saviour, the larger and conventional Bandit, arrived too late to save the sinking enterprise. Designed with help from John Tojeiro, the Bandit used Ford Anglia components and a well-finished glassfibre body and was aimed squarely at the Austin-Healey Sprite. Only two were made before the firm's demise.

In 1991, an enthusiast began offering replica Berkeley T60 kits.

Above: *The Meadows Friskysport mated Italian design (by Michelotti) with traditional microcar virtues and a sporting slant.*

Frisky

Captain Raymond Flower's microcar, the Frisky, had a lot going for it but had such a chequered career that it never realised its potential. Flower had the prototype designed by Michelotti — an interesting gullwing coupé on a separate ladder chassis. But when the Friskysport was launched in late 1957 by engine makers Henry Meadows, it had more conventional glassfibre open and closed bodies. Initially using the 249cc Villers two-stroke mounted at the rear with a motorbike gearbox, the 328cc Villers became available later and offered 65mph. These models had four wheels, the rear ones with a narrow track which obviated the need for a differential. They sold encouragingly well.

The low-slung Friskysprint, with a 492cc Excelsior engine and a claimed 85mph, never made production, but the Family Three did. This was a three-wheeler with accomodation for four people, using 197cc, then 250cc two-cylinder engines. Production concentrated on three-wheelers after 1961 and a larger version, the Prince, was offered from 1960 with a 324cc or 328cc engine. After its fourth change of premises, Frisky abandoned production in 1964.

Opposite page
The Berkeley was Laurie Bond's best design.
The B65 pictured here squeezed 65mph from just 328cc.

Above: *1957 Peerless had luxury and grand touring ability, but lack of development made it uncompetitive.*

Peerless

John Gordon (later to found Gordon-Keeble) and James Byrnes approached racing car constructor Bernie Rodger to design the Peerless in 1957. He created a not unattractive glassfibre body atop a strong square-section spaceframe, with Triumph TR3 mechanicals mounted within. A top speed of 105mph was claimed for the four-seater, and it sold for the reasonable sum of £1,500.

The prospects looked rosy after a Peerless successfully completed the 1958 Le Mans, but the cars were none-too well finished and the project needed further development, which it never got. 325 cars had been built by the time the firm folded in 1960. Bernie Rodger revised the design and relaunched it as the Warwick later that year, also later with Buick V8 power, but the enterprise lasted only a year.

Chapter Three

Kit Cars of the 1960s

One factor above all others gave kit-form cars their *raison d'être*: any car sold in such form was exempt from purchase tax, the less invasive precursor of VAT. This provided kit cars with a distinct price advantage over production cars, which were of course walloped with a not-inconsiderable premium payable to Her Majesty's Government.

The most attractive aspect of this arrangement was that kits could be sold almost fully-built by the factory, leaving just a few items to be bolted on by the customer. Further, this also exempted the cars from passing 'Type Approval' regulations.

The term 'kit car' was not in fact in common parlance at the beginning of the 1960s: such vehicles were generally referred to as 'component cars', suggesting something altogether more elevated than the 'special' of the 1950s from which most manufacturers were hastily trying to distance themselves.

1963 proved to be a watershed year. The then Chancellor, Reginald Maudling, cut purchase tax on new cars by 50 percent, at a stroke destroying most of the tax advantage of kit-built cars. The specials manufacturers who had been supplying glassfibre bodies for contemporary chassis were hit by a sudden evaporation of demand and most bade a sad farewell to their aspirations to become new Colin Chapmans.

Suddenly, 'proper' mass-produced cars looked better value. In particular, the arrival of the Austin-Healey Sprite, BMC's clever little sports two-seater, had a profound effect. It was better-made, more comfortable and far more sporting than any Ford 10-based special could ever be. At £631, it was also affordable. And, generally speaking, production cars experienced a quantum leap in quality. Even a Mini would run rings around a so-called special-built 'sports car'.

Those manufacturers who could recognise the winds of change adopted a more professional and up-market stance, selling their wares as more purist versions of mass-produced sports cars. This was how names such as Ginetta, Rochdale and Fairthorpe survived the period.

A roll-call of some of the component-form cars available in the mid-sixties clearly indicates the importance of quality in the industry at the time: Elva, Gilbern, Ginetta, Lotus, Rochdale, Tornado, Turner and TVR were the prominent names in 1964. Some of their products, like the TVR Grantura, Lotus Elite and Lotus Elan, are now prized collectors' pieces. Many enthusiasts who today hold the Lotus name in awe might be surprised to learn that their £40,000 Elite was probably built from a kit of parts.

Another trend of the 1960s was the beginning of a long-standing relationship between kit cars and the Mini. Many designers saw the Mini's separate subframe layout (and particularly its self-contained drive train) as the ideal basis for their own designs. It allowed virtually any body shape to be built around it, while the engine could be placed up front, in the middle, or at the back. Probably the first such design was the shortlived front-engined Butterfield of 1961, but it was followed in the same year by the Deep Sanderson 301 and the Ogle SX1000. Dizzy Addicot's DART prototype at the 1964 Racing Car Show launched both the Minijem and the Mini-Marcos. By the end of the 1960s, perhaps the best Mini-based sports cars ever made, the GTM and the Unipower, had made their mark as mid-engined pocket rockets beyond compare.

It cannot be denied, however, that in general the 1960s proved to be a rather barren period for kit cars. Despite the appearance of some of the most attractive and meritorious designs in specialist car history, most firms were lucky if they lasted even a few years. The ephemeral butterflies of the 1960s included Diva, Emery, Heron and Triton — all of them well-built cars with much to commend them. Those that survived, though, were often strong enough to continue well past the end of the decade. Davrian, Fairthorpe, Gilbern, Ginetta and Marcos were the success stories of a cruelly unpredictable era.

The 1960s also launched two specialist firms into a different world: unique in the history of specialist cars, two companies graduated to the status of genuine production manufacturers. These were TVR, who stopped making kit-form cars when they launched the more serious Tuscan V8; and Lotus, for whom the Seven — on which their early success was based — had become an embarrassment by 1973. During the late 1960s, Lotus' sales of complete cars had steadily increased; and in 1974, with the arrival of the new Elite, they would abandon the kit car business once and for all.

The sixties had at least seen the amateur-built car industry making great strides, from being the purveyor of simple and often poor-quality glassfibre tubs to a force which came to be taken increasingly seriously. For the customer, that meant better kits which were easier to build and less likely to return to component form. It was something of a golden era, in fact. The people attracted to the breed in those years — both designers and drivers — tended to be genuine enthusiasts.

Toward the end of the decade, there emerged the first murmurings of what was to come in the next. It was something which would change the face of kit cars for ever: the invasion of an idea from America and of a certain floorpan from Germany. The latter was, of course, the Beetle and the object which clothed it was a sort of glassfibre bathtub. The beach buggy was coming to Britain.

The true buggy explosion didn't happen until the 1970s (so its story is reserved for Chapter Five), but it's worth mentioning that the first true *British* buggy, the Volksrod, first putt-putted on UK highways in 1967. Something of this inclination towards light-hearted — indeed, frivolous — transport was already in evidence in the street rod scene. Geoff Jago (later to make more of a mark with a range of kit cars) began advertising the barest GRP tub, described as a Model T Hot Rod, in May 1965. I must admit that street rods are a pet dislike of mine, for which I apologise to erstwhile readers of *Hot Car* (now transmuted into *Performance Car*) who still speak of such names as Ray's Hot Rods, Total Mobility and Mr Ed in tones of hushed respect. I don't! In any event, these early rods really belong to a world beyond the scope of this work, which will not be entered. The only exception is the Neville Trickett-designed Opus HRF, which was only marginally a 'hot rod'.

Above: *1963 Elva Courier 'T'-Type MkIV: a most beautiful sports car whose manufacturers claimed it was 'the only 100mph open two-seater in Europe with fully independent suspension selling for under £1,000'.*

Elva

Elva is one of the most respected of the early sixties specialists, and with good reason. The name itself derives from the French *elle va* ('she goes'), applied to the first racing cars built by garage owner Frank Nichols in 1955. These were successful and popular — particularly in the USA — and demand eventually persuaded Nichols to create a road-going car.

The Courier was built in 1957 and was a handsome beast. It was based around Riley 1500 parts, including the rear suspension and engine. When production began in 1958, however, a variety of engines (including the Wolseley 1500 and MG 1498cc and 1588cc units) had to be used, due to supply difficulties. These MkI cars all had split windscreens and were nearly all exported to America.

Arriving in 1959, the MkII featured a new chassis, one-piece windscreen and better weather equipment. Not until 1960 was the Courier properly available in Britain — as a kit, manufactured in Hastings. The new 1622cc MGA engine propelled the MkII to a top speed above 100mph and from 0 to 60mph in 10 seconds. A coupé version was announced at the 1961 London Racing Car Show.

Elva then suffered a fate which has become commonplace in the precarious world of minor manufacturers. Its American importer, on whom Elva truly depended, failed to pay for a number of cars (he was actually in jail at the time) and in 1961 Elva was forced to liquidate. Courier production passed to Trojan Ltd, who brought it back to life in 1962 as the MkIII with a redesigned chassis and Triumph Herald front suspension. A distinctive reverse-angle notchback hardtop was also offered. Later that year came the 2+2 MkIV roadster and a fastback MkIV coupé. But these cars suffered from chassis problems and had poor-quality bodies.

In 1963, the 'T'-Type MkIV Courier was launched. It was a significant advance for Elva, having Tru-Trak independent rear suspension — unusual for the time. All-independent suspension followed. With the 1798cc MGB engine in place, about 107mph was attainable — with even more performance from the optional Ford Cortina GT unit.

Thereafter, however, Trojan's interest in the Courier waned and the project was taken on in 1965 by Ken Sheppard Sports Cars, who built only the MkIV 'T'-Type 1800 roadster. Over the next couple of years, just 26 more cars were made. Total production of all Elvas exceeded 2,000.

There were two other Elva cars: the Elva-BMW (see Chapter Four) and the Elva 3000, also known as the Cougar. This was a radically redesigned MkIV coupé which housed a three-litre Ford V6. Sadly, only one had been made by the time the Elva marque retired, gracefully, in 1968.

Below: *Fairthorpe's career began with bizarre microcars like this 1958 Atomota, sold complete or in kit form. Not one survives today.*

Fairthorpe

As a marque, Air Vice-Marshal Don 'Pathfinder' Bennett's Fairthorpe spanned the generations, lasting in theory into the 1980s. But it was always an 'awkward sister' in the specialist world, offering everything from exceptionally bad microcars to larger-engined sports coupés. Refinement was always a low priority, and aesthetics were non-existent. Coupled with the fact that Fairthorpe never really publicised itself, it's no surprise that the marque's heyday came when the buying public's tastes were cruder, during the late 1950s and early 1960s.

After the unbearable Atom (1954-1957) and Atomota (1958-60) — the former was once nominated in *Car* magazine as 'the world's worst car' — Fairthorpe tried to better the GRP specials norm with the 1956 Electron sports car on its own chassis with a Coventry-Climax sohc engine allowing up to 110mph. Only 30 were made before production ceased in 1965.

In 1957 came the budget version, the Electron Minor, easily the most successful Fairthorpe. With a 948cc Standard engine, it wasn't fast, but it was popular. Spitfire engine versions followed in 1963. But it was a casualty of Austin's Sprite, and early sales success slowly waned.

Amazingly, the Minor reached a MkVI version and stumbled on until 1974. In all, about 500 were made, plus about 20 2+2 Electrina saloons.

Based on the Electron shell came a range of larger sports cars, beginning with the 1960 Zeta. This was a fearsome Ford Zephyr 2.5-litre-engined beast, which combination convinced about 20 customers to throw caution to the winds. The Rockette of 1963-1967 initially featured three headlamps, one sitting in the middle of the bonnet. A Triumph Vitesse six-cylinder engine sat underneath it. Only 25 were made.

Fairthorpe might have faded away but for the input of the Air Vice-Marshal's son, Torix, who in 1965 developed a wedgey open two-seater called the TX1. It attracted comment through its unique trailing link and transverse rod independent rear suspension, which made the wheels toe in on cornering. Favourable reaction encouraged Fairthorpe to launch the TX-GT in 1967, now sporting coupé bodywork and Triumph GT6 power in place of the 1500cc Cortina unit in the prototype.

Above: *The definitive Fairthorpe was the Electron Minor (right), but a range of larger-engined models like the Zeta (left) were fiery and often frightening machines.*

Available alongside the TX-GT from 1968 was the restyled, lower-slung TX-S with no opening rear hatch and more glass. TX models could now be fitted with Spitfire engines and, from 1971, with the introduction of the 'luxury' TX-SS, Triumph 2.5 PI units. With the TR6 version of this engine fitted, a top speed of 130mph was claimed. The TX range sold around 50 in total, the last in 1976.

Torix Bennett went on to form his own marque, TX, to make the whacky Tripper buggy (see Chapter Five). But Fairthorpe itself did not die. In the late 1980s, two enthusiasts bought the old Denham works and created the Motorville Pathfinder, a 'new' Fairthorpe with the flavour of an Electron. Sold in kit form, it used Cortina mechanicals in two-seat and 2+2 guises and is still available at the time of writing.

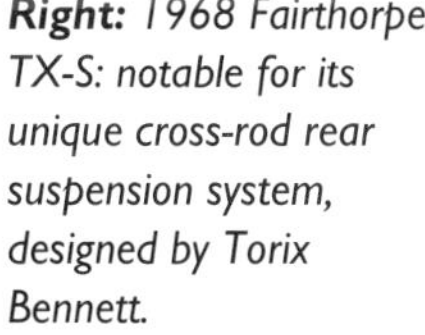

Right: *1968 Fairthorpe TX-S: notable for its unique cross-rod rear suspension system, designed by Torix Bennett.*

Above: *1960 Gilbern GT: not especially pretty, this Welsh 2+2 was a strong seller due to its good performance and low price.*

Gilbern

Wales has few sports cars of which to be proud, but it was the birthplace of the Gilbern marque. Founded by butcher Giles Smith and German-born Bernard Friese, whose compounded names gave the company its title, Gilbern launched its first model, the GT, in 1959.

Initially sold as a bare body/chassis kit, the Gilbern quickly became available only in complete component form. A choice of engines was offered: the 948cc Sprite (with the option of a supercharger), the 1098cc Coventry-Climax, or the 1558cc MGA. As of 1963, the MGB 1798cc engine was standardised and the model renamed the 1800 GT.

Quickly established as a quality sports car, it was cheap at just £945 and was a genuine 100+mph four-seater, even if not a particularly pretty one. By the time it was discontinued in 1967, nearly 400 had been delivered.

Its successor was the upmarket Genie of 1966, with either 2.5 or three-litre Ford V6 engines. It retained the GT's chassis, but in strengthened form — a point Giles Smith would demonstrate by swinging his weight on the chassis-mounted doors. Sharper styling helped towards sales of 197 cars by the Genie's demise in 1969, but its harsh ride and whippy chassis didn't. The Invader which replaced it — of which more in Chapter Six — aimed to remedy these faults.

Deep Sanderson

Morgan tuner and racer Chris Lawrence founded Deep Sanderson in 1960, acknowledging his backer, Sanderson, and his jazz hero, Deep Henderson. The marque was the most successful manufacturing venture for Lawrence — though that isn't saying much for a man whose troubled career exemplified the attitude immortalised by Robert the Bruce: if at first you don't succeed...

After unhappy attempts at Formula Junior Cars, Lawrence built the 301 prototype in 1961 — a hideous Mini-Cooper rear-engined car nicknamed the 'perfume delivery wagon'. Restyled for its 1963 launch, only 14 were sold. Typical of his fortunes, Lawrence made a loss on each and every one of them and, at his two Le Mans outings in 301s, the cars either crashed or broke down. Returning from the 1964 event, he had a bad accident which effectively spelt the end of 301 production.

Lawrence went on to make two more racing prototypes, the 302 and 303, neither of which had any success. He was also involved with the Jack Pearce F1 affair, which never came to anything. And as for the Monica grand tourer, for which he made all the prototypes, the whole unfortunate saga is related in Chapter Six.

Above: *Racing driver turned constructor Chris Lawrence had a luckless history with his sports cars.*

Below: *Lawrence's 1963 Deep Sanderson 301: a short and troubled life.*

Ginetta

Ginetta is one of the select few British specialists to have remained, until recently, in constant solvency and is unique in having remained a family business, run by the Walklett brothers, until their retirement in 1989.

Ginetta offered its first model, the Lotus Six-style G2, in 1957, and supplemented it with the more substantial G3 in 1959. Total production of Ginettas had exceeded 100 by 1960, but it was not until the following year, with the G4, that the marque really got into its stride. The fact that this has become far and away the most collectable Ginetta hints at how good it was. Based on a spaceframe chassis, the GRP-bodied sports car used double wishbone and coilsprung front suspension with a live rear axle. The standard engine was the 997cc Ford Anglia unit.

The G4 progressed with coupé, Series II (1963), lightweight G4R (1964) and Series III (1966) versions, the last with a new space-frame and pop-up headlamps. Ford engines of 1.2 and 1.3 litres were options and the 1498cc Ford Cortina GT-engined version became known as the G5, albeit briefly — the name caused too much confusion. And the G6 was a limited run of DKW-engined G4s for Germany.

Total G4 production had exceeded 500 by the time it was retired in 1969. But this was not the end of the G4: it was revived in 1981 in Series IV guise and was subsequently modified, as will be seen in later chapters, to become the G27 and G33.

The Walklett brothers also tried their hand at a large-engined sports car for the American market. The G10 of 1965 had a Ford 4.7-litre V8 and sported attractive bodywork which used MGB doors and windscreen. It was supply problems with the MG parts, coupled with the model's non-homologation, which killed the G10 after only six had been made, four coupés and two convertibles. The same supply problems plagued the MGB-engined G10-based G11 which, despite its attractive kit price, died after a run of just 12 cars.

Left: *1961 Ginetta G4: the definitive Ginetta and the car on which the marque's fortunes were founded. Today the G4 is highly collectable.*

Below: *Ginetta G15: the best-selling model in Ginetta's history and a fine handler and performer.*

Right: *1967 Cox GTM: the first mid-engined kit ever offered, and one of the best, it used Mini subframes front and rear.*

The G4-based G12 was a pure race machine, though cars were also modified for road use. The G12 was revived in America in the 1980s, much to the chagrin of the Walklett brothers. Ginetta's new Scunthorpe-based owners also put a road version of the G12 into production in 1990, intended primarily for the Japanese market.

It was the G15 which was Ginetta's most successful model and which, ironically, almost led to the company's downfall. Introduced in 1967, the glassfibre G15 was a semi-monocoque two-seater coupé which used a rear-mounted Hillman Imp Sport engine, offering about 100mph top speed and frugal fuel consumption.

Several motorsport victories helped the popularity of the G15. So did its low component-form price of £799. Healthy sales led the Walkletts to leave their base in Witham, Essex, in 1972, and move into larger premises in Suffolk. The expansion was too rapid, however, and to avoid bankruptcy they were obliged to return to Witham.

The G15 was dropped in 1974, largely a victim of VAT and the necessity of selling complete cars rather than kits. 794 had been made — an impressive tally for such a small firm. But, with its demise, the company's heyday was ended. Only the G21, introduced in 1970, was left to carry Ginetta's road-going colours unsteadily through the next decade.

GTM

Probably the first mid-engined kit ever offered was the GTM, made by Cox & Co from late 1966. The initials stood for Grand Touring Mini, indicating the use of Mini subframes front and rear, so that the engine was mounted amidships.

Of semi-monocoque steel and glassfibre construction, it was a dumpy little two-seater with distinctive flying buttress rear styling. Cox sold the GTM in kit form, but quality and development were lacking. Even so, 55 cars had been sold when the project was taken over in 1968 by Howard Heerey. Heerey redesigned many aspects of the GTM, making it more luxurious and better developed. But his firm went under in 1972, by which time a further 250 cars had been produced.

Now the GTM moved to Hartlepool, where it lay dormant until purchased by KMB Autosports in 1976. Uprated, it took three further years to re-enter production.

In 1980, it finally passed to GTM Cars of Loughborough, where it has remained in production averaging sales of around 60 a year. A Richard Oakes-designed 2+2 convertible, the Rossa, was added in 1986. GTM was further strengthened by its acquisition, in 1991, of the Midas and NG projects.

Left: *One of a string of GRP shells from Rochdale, the GT was its most successful with almost 800 sales.*

Below: *The curvaceous lines and sound engineering of the Rochdale Olympic (here in Phase II guise) led to its being dubbed the 'British Porsche'.*

Rochdale

Rochdale was not only one of the most successful kit car firms of the 1950s and 1960s but something of a pioneer in the use of glassfibre in cars, a fact which is seldom appreciated. During its 20-plus years, it sold almost 1,500 cars and bodyshells.

Founded in 1948, Rochdale's first road car project began in 1952 as a very basic GRP shell. During the 1950s, several models were offered: the Type C, Type F, MkVI and ST. Its most successful model was the pretty GT, for Ford E93A chassis, in open form called the Riviera. Nearly 800 of these sports shells were built at the Rochdale factory.

But by far the most important Rochdale was the Olympic, which first appeared in 1959. After the Lotus Elite of 1957, it was only the second GRP monocoque car ever to be made in series. Production began in 1960, with the engine and many mechanical parts taken from the Riley 1.5 or, in more basic form, with Ford 8 or 10 engines. It was a superior kit car, soundly engineered and prettily styled; *Motor Sport* called it 'a British Porsche'. With the twin-carb Riley engine fitted, a top speed of over 100mph was attainable.

A factory fire almost nipped the Olympic in the bud. New moulds had to be taken from cars parked outside the factory in order for production to continue. Total production of 'Phase I' Olympics was about 150.

The Phase II arrived in 1962 with an opening rear hatch and Ford 997cc or 1498cc Cortina GT power (although Riley and MGA engines could also be fitted). Triumph Spitfire front suspension replaced the Riley set-up and the new 115mph Olympic was showered with praise from the press.

Around 250 Phase II Olympics had been sold by the time kit production ceased in 1968, after which Rochdale concentrated on industrial glassfibre work. The company continued to offer body/chassis units and bodyshells to eager individuals on a special-order basis until at least 1977.

Unipower GT

One of the best specialist cars ever produced in Britain was the Unipower GT. This attractively-styled two-seater represented the zenith of Mini-based sports cars in the 1960s.

The mid-engined space-frame design was taken on by tractor manufacturers, Universal Power Drives, who took the aluminium prototype and developed the production version in glassfibre. Reaction to the 1966 debut of the Unipower was enthusiastic. With universal double wishbone and coil spring independent suspension, the 40.5in-high car was endowed with exceptional cornering abilities. Thanks to a slender 10.25cwt weight, performance was spirited, too. With the smaller 998cc Mini-Cooper engine in place, 105mph was possible; with the 1275cc Cooper engine, up to 120mph was quoted, and 0-60mph came in eight seconds. This made it a popular competition car — and popular with the motoring press which, unusually for a kit-form car, conducted road tests of the Unipower which were glowing in their praise.

By 1968, when the project was taken over by a new firm, UWF, about 60 cars had been made. Only a year and 15 cars later, the company had ceased trading.

There were other, peripheral Unipowers: the extraordinary Quasar-Unipower (see Chapter Nine) was one; plans for a Peter Bohanna-designed MkII Unipower using a BMC 2.2-litre six-cylinder engine were scotched, although the idea later surfaced as the Diablo from Bohanna Stables; and a Triumph Stag-engined Unipower project was lost with UWF's liquidation.

Below: *1966 Unipower GT: low, fast and a superb driving machine, the mid-engined Unipower was one of the best of all kit cars.*

Above: *Just what were this Opus HRF and anoraked woman doing on a windswept British beach? Curious publicity shot.*

Opus HRF

An unholy alliance between entrepreneur Geoff Thomas and budding designer Neville Trickett brought about a car unique in the specialist field. Although called the Opus HRF (Hot Rod Ford), it was never really welcomed in street rodding circles and was always a 'marginal' among kit cars. Its biggest recommendation was Trickett's involvement — he went on to found the celebrated Siva marque.

In 1964, Thomas and Trickett had worked together to make the Minisprint, a roof-and-body chop on Minis. The Opus was an entirely new departure and a curious hotch-potch of influences: Ford Popular and Anglia suspension, Cortina 1600 engine, Mini front wheels and a sort of Model T 'bucket', as bodyshells were called in hot rod circles. Launched in 1966, it immediately earned a reputation for having precarious road manners. *Autocar* tested one and commented: 'The Opus belongs to a previous generation... One recalls those epic thrills, like spinning through somebody's hedge.' But, with the body/chassis unit priced at £99, many were prepared to be tolerant.

Weighing only 8cwt, the Opus was claimed to reach 60mph from rest in just seven seconds. People actually started buying them, many forming the basis of drag-racing specials, and production rapidly reached one a week.

Jim Clark, Stirling Moss and even Colin Chapman had drives in the Opus, presumably to extend their skills to the full! But by 1969, after selling 200 kits, the original purveyors had lost interest. A rescue bid by a firm called Lambert relaunched the Opus in 1970, but two years later only 20 more had been sold: the old Opus pocus had faded. Uncomfortably straddling the hot rod and beach buggy worlds, it no longer had any real market to exploit.

Chapter Four

Low-production and Coachbuilt Cars of the 1960s

The sixties was a decisive decade for firms about to hit the specialist 'big time'. Lotus and TVR cemented their respective fortunes with a string of increasingly professional models. Both firms sold the majority of their cars in kit form during the sixties, but both made moves upmarket. TVR made the break from kit-form cars in the mid-sixties, Lotus in the early seventies. Reliant made its fortune in the sixties, too, with a new range of sports cars.

But there were still very few British companies trying to compete with the establishment. One reason was that the market was already crowded in the days before the giant corporations had gobbled up the small fry. Still around at the start of the decade were such names as Alvis, Armstrong-Siddeley and Lea-Francis, all of them soon to disappear. Another reason was that even the big names such as Jaguar and Aston Martin were then highly exclusive because of their low production levels: why should customers risk an unknown manufacturer?

There were attempts, but all of them were unsuccessful: the Gordon-Keeble was a brave try, while the Gitane and GSM were too ambitious.

As the bigger names ducked out, were eaten, or grew into something different, there opened up a market for something more specialist. Marcos was the sole name which succeeded in growing through the 1960s with its unique and advanced sports cars, but even they came a cropper just one year into the next decade. Ogle made a successful foray into car manufacture, but that was effectively over by the mid-sixties and it became a simple styling house.

Apart from a smattering of British microcars (almost all killed off by 1965), that was that for the sixties: a particularly barren period for specialist car makers, though the profusion of the following decade was to tell a rather different story...

Delta

Due to its racing success in Britain during 1960, the South African GSM Dart was known over here before its founders decided to set up production in the UK. Launched at the 1961 Racing Car Show, and renamed the GSM Delta, the car had a very complete specification at £1,250.

Using tooling from Cape Town, the Delta's construction was simple: a ladder chassis, with subframes carrying the transverse leaf spring front suspension and rigid Ford 100E axle with trailing arms at the rear, plus a glassfibre open or coupé sports body. Ford 105E Anglia power was the standard fitment, with tuning options up to 90bhp (although the Delta was too heavy for outstanding performance).

Founder Bob van Niekerk scored some successes in the works competition car, while Jeff Uren won many class victories in international events. Its racing bias meant it wasn't a very comfortable road car.

An ambitious production rate and the development of a coupé version (some of which were built) led to financial trouble and the firm folded in late 1961 after 35 Deltas had been made. Van Niekerk returned to South Africa to restart production there in 1962.

Gordon-Keeble

After John Gordon's experience with the Peerless, he decided to build a grand tourer of greater quality which would undercut the products of the established marques. His ambitious plans were very nearly successful.

Jim Keeble worked on the chassis, while Giorgetto Giugiaro (then with Bertone) was enlisted to style the steel body. Appearing at the 1960 Geneva Motor Show, the Gordon GT (as it was then known) had a sophisticated specification. The spaceframe chassis followed Peerless principles with square section steel members and double wishbone independent suspension fore and de Dion aft. The Gordon was fitted with a 4.6-litre Chevrolet V8, claimed to take the car to 140mph. But finance never materialised for the project and, despite Armstrong-Siddeley showing an interest, Gordon's company was wound up in 1961 without a production run.

But a new company was formed in 1964 to make the car, now renamed the Gordon-Keeble GK1. The body was now in glassfibre (made by Williams & Pritchard) and the 5367cc Corvette engine replaced the discontinued Chevy 4.6, giving it even better performance.

Fine handling, a luxurious interior and hand-finishing looked almost too good a deal at only £2,798 — which indeed it was, as the cars were labour-intensive to build and the firm lost money on them. By 1965, the firm collapsed, having made 93 cars.

Too good to die, the project was bought and restarted within two months. Slightly redesigned and renamed the Gordon-Keeble IT, it was priced more realistically at £3,989 and consequently sold less well: in fact, just six were made before the firm's demise in 1967.

American John de Bruyne bought a damaged GK1 and attempted to update the GT in 1968, mostly with masses of chrome. The de Bruyne Motor Car Co of Newmarket, Suffolk exhibited its GT at the 1968 New York Motor Show (alongside its mid-engined sports car, which borrowed components from the GK1), but only two cars of the Gordon-Keeble type ever bore the de Bruyne badge.

Apart from one car built up from spares in 1972, that was that for the Gordon-Keeble, perhaps the only specialist car ever to have given Jensen, Bristol and Aston Martin a run for their money.

Elva

By 1964, Elva was in the hands of Trojan, but founder Frank Nichols, now more concerned with the competition side of the operation, had plans to make a fabulous mid-engined GT.

A Mk7S sports-racer was despatched to coachbuilders Fissore of Italy in 1964 to be rebodied in aluminium according to a Trevor Fiore design. It made its debut at the 1964 Turin Motor Show. Two more bodies were made by Fissore, and the car appeared at the London Motor Show the same year, priced at £4,500.

The Elva-BMW GT160, as the car was called, was beautiful to behold, thanks to the skills of Fiore. But its promise was never to be realised. It was too heavy and its 125bhp BMW 1800 engine stumped up a top speed of only 125mph. Trojan was feeling edgy about the whole Elva concern and sold one of the two unfinished cars off (it raced at Le Mans as the fastest British car in 1965).

Above: *South African-designed GSM Delta had a short but sweet production run.*

Below: *Italian styling, an American engine and British engineering made a promising cocktail in the Gordon-Keeble, but production costs were too high.*

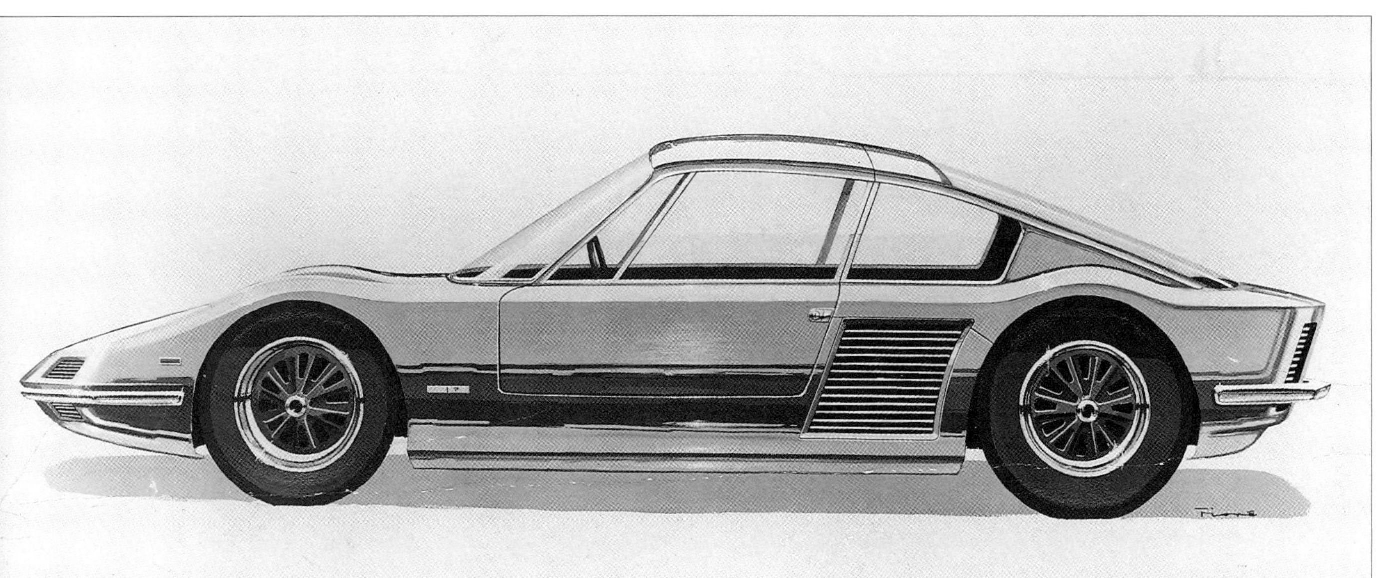

Above: *Trevor Fiore's final styling drawing for the gorgeous but ill-fated Elva-BMW GT160.*

Opposite page
Top: *1960 Ogle 1.5: a curious attempt at a stylish GT based on a Riley 1.5 platform.*

Bottom: *1961 Ogle SX1000: probably the best specification ever offered in a Mini-based specialist car — a car which worked very well.*

Ken Sheppard acquired the Elva marque in 1965 and planned to put the GT160 into production. Selling the BMW 1800-engined car on, he modified the third and last GT160 with a 3.5-litre Buick V8. Called the 160XS, it was claimed to top 150mph but was apparently a monster to drive. Sheppard hoped to market the 160XS in kit form with a glassfibre body but the plan was scotched.

Ogle

David Ogle set up his design company in 1954, making a living designing TVs and radios. His first vehicle project, with which he hoped to beat the Italian masters at their own game, was begun in 1959.

The Ogle 1.5 appeared in 1960. Its tubby four-seater glassfibre body (complete with little fins) sat on a Riley 1.5 platform reinforced by a tubular structure developed by Tojeiro. The engine and suspension were standard Riley 1.5: 68bhp and not a lot of performance. Only eight were made before David Ogle's death in 1962 at the wheel of his next car project, the SX1000.

The SX1000 prototype appeared in December 1961 and was one of the first attempts to rebody the Mini. As such, BMC were awkward in supplying cars, so Ogle had to buy complete Mini vans retail and replace their bodywork with his own bulbous glassfibre coachwork and luxurious interior; alternatively, he would convert customers' Minis for £550. BMC eventually relented in 1962 on the condition that the car was renamed the Ogle Mini. The most powerful 1275 Cooper 'S' engined cars could reach 110mph.

But Ogle's death and the high cost of making the car ended production in 1963, after 66 had been made. The SX1000 moulds were sold in 1966 to boatbuilders Norman Fletcher Ltd and the car was rather unpleasantly restyled, front and rear. The Fletcher GT lasted just one year and a mere four cars were built.

Control at Ogle was assumed by Czech-born Tom Karen, who continued the motoring side of the business with the SX250, a pretty rebodying of the Daimler SP250 (which eventually became the Reliant Scimitar in 1964). In 1965, it presented the Triplex GTS, a glass estate version of the SX250, which it offered as the Ogle GTE for a £750 premium over the Reliant. Ogle also went on to design Reliant's Scimitar GTE, the Bond Bug, Reliant's Robin and Kitten and the Triplex Princess Estate. Its last production car was the Ogle Aston Martin of 1972 (see Chapter Six). Ogle also built a full-size one-off of Meccano's 'M' toy in 1975, called the Mogul!

Peel

The Isle of Man's most famous car maker was Peel Engineering, a firm engaged in all sorts of unusual automotive projects. The first was the Manxman of 1955, a crude three-wheeled microcar with rotating doors which was one of the first kit-form cars. This was followed by the P1000, a brick-like glassfibre shell for Ford Pop chassis and a GRP replica Mini shell.

Peel's most celebrated product was the P50, which appeared in 1962. This was perhaps the world's shortest car — a mere 4ft 5in long. A single-seater three-wheeler, the P50's 49cc engine powered it to a top speed of 38mph — a frightening experience, by all accounts, as the P50 was prone to toppling over (there were even little runners built in for this eventuality).

The two-seater Trident had a transparent bubble top which tilted forward for entry. Like the P50, it had no reverse gear and came equipped with a handle on its rump. About 100 Peel micros were made.

Peel's last model was the Trident Mini, a bulbous little GRP coupé for Mini mechanicals. Introduced at the 1966 Racing Car Show, only two were built before Peel sold out to Bill Last's Viking Performance, of Suffolk. Last made a further 20 or so under the name Viking Minisport before his involvement with the Trident (see elsewhere in this chapter) edged it into the twilight.

Marcos

The name Marcos was a composite of two illustrious characters of specialist motoring, Jem Marsh and Frank Costin. Marsh was making the Speedex range of glassfibre specials when, in 1959, he met Frank Costin, ace aerodynamicist who had worked with Lotus, Vanwall and Lister.

The first Marcos, known as the Marcos GT, was conceived as a grand touring car which could take to the race-circuits if required. Costin's experience with wood in aircraft design persuaded him to build the GT as a monocoque almost entirely of wood (the nose cone was glassfibre). The prototype of 1959 used a Ford 100E sidevalve engine, but production models began with Ford 105E and, later, Ford Classic 1340cc engines.

Marsh and Bill Moss raced Marcos GTs with tremendous success through 1960. Moss took nine wins in nine starts, the Autosport Championship was won outright by John Sutton with a Costin-type Marcos, and the then-unknown Jackie Stewart cut his teeth on a GT. Orders started to flood in.

The GT was an exceptionally ugly coupé with gullwing doors and frog-eye headlamps, which made it unattractive as a road car. (There were customers for them, however; Marsh remembers driving to Glasgow and personally delivering Jackie Stewart's GT.) On the plus side, its modified Triumph Herald front suspension and Ford live rear axle with leading arms and a Panhard rod worked very well: these early cars were known both as 'wooden wonders' and 'ugly ducklings'.

Brothers Dennis and Peter Adams joined Marcos in 1960, Dennis restyling the GT with a smooth bonnet, one-piece windscreen and cleaner rear end, which used more glassfibre panels; Costin left at this time, reportedly unhappy at the use of so much GRP. The gullwing GT went on to sell 29 examples.

Work began on a rather prettier Marcos in 1962. The Adams brothers designed and built the Spyder, an open sports car, but potential customers all wanted a hard-top, so it remained unique. The Spyder was modified into a fastback coupé in 1963, again using a wooden monocoque chassis but with rather more glassfibre in the bodywork. 25 were made by 1964.

Around the same time, Dennis Adams had built an extraordinary machine called the XP. With sliding doors, a central driving position and a profile that wouldn't have looked out of place in *Thunderbirds*, it was revolutionary and could have become a Marcos, had not Jem Marsh decided on developing another pure road car.

Dennis Adams designed the new Marcos in 1963 and, at its debut at the 1964 Racing Car Show, it stole the honours. A futuristic glassfibre body sat on the familiar Marcos wooden chassis. The original intention had been to create an 'all-new' car with its own tailor-made suspension; financial constraints led to Triumph wishbones being used on the front, although a novel de Dion rear end with Triumph arms was fitted. Even this, however, was later changed to a Ford live axle set-up.

Marsh opted for the Volvo 1800cc engine and the car was christened the Marcos 1800. With 96bhp on tap, a top speed of 115mph was attainable — or more from the optional enlarged 2-litre unit. The price in 1965 was £1,885 in kit form.

Right: *Probably the world's smallest car, the Peel P50 single-seater, made in the Isle of Man, was nothing if not entertaining to drive.*

Below: *Extraordinary bulges and wobbles graced Peel's last attempt at a road car, the Trident Mini of 1966.*

Bottom: *Jem Marsh stands beside the very first Marcos, the all-wooden prototype of 1959. It was called Xylon, the Greek word for 'wood'.*

In 1965, after 106 had been made, Marsh changed the engine to the Ford Cortina 1500 unit. Easier servicing was offset by a lack of power (82bhp) and production amounted to only 82. There was a bored-out 120bhp 1650cc Chris Lawrence engine available from 1967, but the Marcos 1650 was unreliable, keeping production down to 32 cars. In 1967, the 1600cc Ford crossflow engine replaced the 1500, and, with a build total of 192, this finally brought volume production to Marcos Cars.

A powerful engine was what the Marcos had always cried out for, so in 1968 Marsh installed a Ford 3-litre V6 in the same classic shell, good enough for 125mph. Complete cars sold for £2,350, or £1,790 in kit form.

With Marsh's eyes very much on America, an all-new steel chassis was developed after about 100 wooden-chassis 3-litres had been made. This had a beneficial effect on costs and made the cars easier to market, but Marsh had to change the engine — for US laws — to the Volvo 164 3-litre unit, which offered similar performance to the Ford. About 250 were made. There were also 11 cars fitted with Triumph 2.5-litre engines, six metal-chassis cars with the Ford 1600 engine, and about 40 of the firm's last model, the 2-litre of 1970, which had a Ford V4 engine.

Back-tracking slightly, Marcos also introduced in 1965 the Mini-Marcos, a radical departure from its previous wares. Based on a Paul Emery-designed prototype built in 1964 by Falcon (a parent company of Marcos) for pilot Dizzy Addicot, and called the DART, the Mini-Marcos was a GRP monocoque with Mini subframes bolted in through metal plates, at prices from £199. It was a quite ugly little buzz-box whose main distinction lay in its being the only British car to finish the 1966 Le Mans 24-Hour Race. A tailgate was added in 1971, just as the Marcos name fluttered out. Taken over by Rob Walker, then in 1975 by Harold Dermott's D&H Fibreglass Techniques, production of the Mini-Marcos reached a grand total of about 1,200. In a surprise move, Marsh relaunched the model in MkV guise in 1991, after a Japanese importer had ordered 100.

The Mantis of 1970 was an extraordinary grand tourer, intended as a luxury four-seater Marcos. Its bizarre lines were a rather hacked-about version of Dennis Adams' original sketches and caused much controversy.

A brand-new semi-spaceframe chassis accepted a Triumph TR6 engine, which gave the 20cwt car a top speed of about 125mph. Very well appointed and boasting an unexpectedly good ride, it was available fully-built or in kit form. But only 32 were produced before the firm's temporary demise as a producer of cars in 1971.

That demise was caused partly by the high development cost of the Mantis, but more as the result of a batch of Volvo-engined Marcos 3-litres being stranded in the 'States having failed local regulations. (The Mantis has been revived twice since then: first in 1981 and again in 1986 by Autotune, who renamed it the Mirage.)

Marsh provided servicing and parts for Marcos cars for ten more years but boldly relaunched the two-seater in 1981 with a variety of Ford engines. Other models followed: the Rover V8-powered Mantula which made its first appearance late in 1983, the Mantula Spyder (late 1985), the 2-litre coupé and Spyder (1990) and the Martina (1991), all of them sharing the same basic shape as the classic Adams-penned 1800 of 1963. In 1992, a new chapter was added to the story with the arrival of the fully-built Mantara, a totally new car with different front suspension and a new body shape, which nevertheless retained the familiar Marcos lines. The Mantara had the option of a Rover 4.5-litre engine, giving a top speed of 160mph and a 0-60mph time of under five seconds.

Opposite page
The Marcos 1800 was the archetypal Jem Marsh car, born in 1963 and still in production today with its basic shape intact.

Right: *No-one could call the 1965 Mini-Marcos pretty, but it was endearing. It has since achieved cult status in Japan, so much so that Marcos decided to relaunch the model in 1991.*

Below: *The sole genuine four-seater Marcos was the Mantis of 1970. Weird, but only marginally wonderful, it remained in production only briefly.*

***Above:** The TR6-engined Trident Tycoon had rectangular headlamps as opposed to the other models' inset circular lamps.*

Trident

The Trident started out as a TVR, with Trevor Fiore commissioned to design a luxury model and Fissore of Italy to build it. The TVR Trident made its debut at the 1965 Geneva Motor Show. Two prototypes were built before TVR agent and manufacturer of the Viking Minisport kit, Bill Last, instigated the construction of a third, drophead, version.

TVR went under in 1965 and Last took on the Trident himself. Developed by Fissore during 1966, the Trident was launched the following year as a 2+2 coupé or convertible based on an Austin-Healey box-section chassis. With its 390bhp 4.7-litre Ford V8, it was claimed to reach 142mph and power from 0-60mph in just five seconds! Handling it was a job for the brave, or foolish. A rather more sensible Ford 3-litre V6 version joined it later in 1967.

Trident standardised the fitment of a lengthened TR6 chassis from 1969, as production of the Austin-Healey had ended. The Trident Car Co introduced names for its models: the 4.7-litre model became the Clipper and the V6 became the Venturer.

The range was revised in 1971, the Clipper now having its headlamps mounted in its grille (as opposed to recessed as before) and costing £4,113. In late 1971, the Clipper got a 5549cc Chrysler V8, with 300bhp on tap, and was joined by the Triumph TR6-engined Tycoon at the same time, born as a result of supply difficulties from Ford strikes. Few were sold before the firm collapsed in 1972, only to be revived by a subsidiary of Last's which carried things on rather more quietly until 1974. About 225 Tridents of all types had been made.

With American backing, the project was relaunched in 1976. Two models were offered: the V6 Venturer and the Clipper, which now boasted a Ford 6-litre engine. These revivals had impact bumpers and quad headlamps. Despite the ambitious plans of the Trident Motor Company, no more than 10 were finished before the firm's collapse in mid-1977. The Trident never got the success its beauty deserved.

TVR Tina

Reformed after its 1965 hiccough, Martin Lilley's new regime at TVR allowed itself a strange aberration in 1966: the TVR Tina. Again using the talents of designer Trevor Fiore and coachbuilders Fissore, the Tina was a steel-bodied 2+2 convertible mated to an Imp Sport floorpan. The following year, the Sypder was joined by a fastback coupé version with revised front-end treatment.

At a projected price of £998 plus taxes, the Tina simply wasn't an economical proposition for TVR. In any case, just what the company thought it was doing with a small rear-engined car which could hardly reach 100mph is anybody's guess.

WSM

The WSM series was built by Douglas Wilson-Spratt and Jim McManus. Their first car, the WSM Sprite GT, was built in 1961 for rallying purposes, but sired a production run with American finance from 1962.

The alloy bodywork was based on an Austin-Healey Sprite floorpan, strengthened with a tubular spaceframe sub-structure. Most had GRP bonnets but two racers were built completely in glassfibre. After a sporadic production run ending in 1967, a total of 24 had been made.

WSM's other projects, rebodied versions of the Austin-Healey 3000, MG 1100 and MGB GT, never reached production and remained unique.

Ikenga

Few specialist projects are as unusual as the Ikenga. On the one hand, it seemed professionally styled (by its creator, American born David Gittens), beautifully constructed (by Williams & Pritchard) and finely engineered (with help from Ken Sheppard). On the other, it was obviously under-developed and over-hyped.

Sheppard had sold Gittens a McLaren M6 Can-Am chassis on which he proceeded to create his Ikenga (which means either a two-horned mythical beast or 'a man's life force', depending on whose true-or-bluff you accept). McLaren mechanicals were hardly suitable for daily driving, so a Chevrolet Camaro Z-28 engine and ZF five-speed gearbox were substituted.

The first body shape was an ungainly block with a forward-hingeing canopy, but this was much improved with a hingeing one-piece front body section built by Radford. The Ikenga debuted at Harrods in 1968 to a furore of press coverage. It even got on to television's *Blue Peter*.

Some of its curious (and probably fictitious) features included fluid-filled instruments, a distance proximity sensor, rear view TV camera and a Perspex boot lid which optimistically doubled up as an air brake.

Gittens quoted some highly speculative performance figures for the 325bhp projectile: 162mph, 0-60mph in five seconds and 0-100mph in 11.5. He even intended pursuing a limited production run of 50 cars, each priced at £9,000, although where his supply of McLaren chassis was to come from is a mystery.

Gittens joined Radford before returning to America and the Ikenga was left high and dry. Today, it is a resident of the Manx Motor Museum.

Below: *1967 TVR Tina prototypes were a blind-alley departure for TVR.*

Above: *1962 WSM Sprite GT: very pretty alloy-bodied coupé based on the Austin-Healey Sprite.*

Below: *The McLaren M6-based Ikenga was reputed to have cost £75,000 to build, but the whole project was a victim of huge over-hyping.*

Chapter Five

Of Buggies and Fun Cars: Kit Cars of the 1970s

The swinging sixties, which turned out to be not all that swinging as far as cars in general were concerned, left one far-out shoot growing in the specialist garden which proliferated into the automotive equivalent of a field of puff-ball mushrooms: a huge explosion of peculiar-shaped objects.

That shoot was the beach buggy, an American idea which migrated to just about everywhere on the globe. The clammy coasts and foggy interior of Britain made it just about the unlikeliest place possible for an outcrop of these wild Beetle-based creations. In desert-dusted America, the notion made sense. On the beach in Clacton, it was a wash-out.

Nevertheless, over the years 1968-1971 a flourishing trade in metalflake glassfibre tubs grew up. Almost all were rip-offs of the GP Buggy, itself based on the Meyers Manx, the first-ever dune buggy born in the States, which invented the classic buggy shape. John Jobber's GP was (and still is) the most successful British buggy, although the honour of being first in the UK belongs probably to the Volksrod.

A massive industry supported such names as Seaspray, Dingbat, UFO, Doodlebug, Tripper, and others equally far-fetched. Reaching its crazy height in the summer of 1971, the boom evaporated almost overnight later that year as people realised that actually driving these things was a fairly unpleasant experience and that building them was often near-impossible. Quality was not a high priority for most buggy makers.

The arrival of the buggy, and its sudden fashionability, persuaded a whole new generation of designers to experiment wildly. Champions of the 1970s were Barrie Stimson, with a whole succession of outrageous contraptions, Neville

Trickett, with his Siva Marque, and Richard Oakes, whose career began at the turn of the decade with the Tramp beach buggy.

All sorts of weird vehicles popped out of Britain's lock-ups, but to objective onlookers it was obvious that such inventive but impractical devices could not remain popular for long. Along with everything else, the introduction of VAT in 1973 drove the final nail into their coffin, along with many other more sober kit cars.

The firms that survived make interesting reading. GP was big enough to continue selling its buggies and other VW-based cars; Dutton's formula of cheap Lotus Seven-style roadsters was a winner; Jago's Geep proved to be immensely popular; and the only two 'classically styled' kits, the RMB Gentry and the Spartan, went on to sell in huge numbers.

The great casualties were not only the fun cars but also, ultimately, the imaginative designers. Such advanced designs as the Nova, the Futura and the Voodoo had a rough time of it. In their day, they were ahead of the major manufacturers, but as technology advanced the low-budget sculptures of the specialist designers could no longer keep pace. Flush-fitting glass, for instance, now standard on any new car, is far too expensive for any kit firm to contemplate.

The situation was so dîre that many commentators predicted the demise of the kit car, and for a while during the mid-1970s it looked as though they were right. Sales plummeted, the quality of most of what was on offer was often very poor, design standards fell, and the number of models available dropped almost to extinction — down to about 30, in 1977.

The first inklings of change emerged in the last two years of the decade. Designers like Richard Oakes and William Towns became active with rather more practical cars than kit car owners had been used to. Oakes' Midas, Towns' Hustler and Trickett's Madison paved the way.

There was also the welcome beginning of a trend towards high-quality upmarket kits. Lynx began offering its delectable D-Type replica in kit form, for example, in a trend which caught fire in the 1980s.

With hindsight, the 1970s was something of a 'mixed bag' for kit cars. On the one hand, it can be seen as the most adventurous period in kit car history, and certainly the craziest. On the other hand, it witnessed the virtual decimation of the genre. But, to the author's mind, some of the most fascinating and humorous cars of all were born during the 1970s... along with all of the most ridiculously named!

Left: *An extra row of seats made the long-wheelbase VW Super Buggy more practical and easier to build, since it fitted an unshortened VW floorpan.*

GP

One would hardly expect a firm engaged in the preparation of sports racers such as Ford GT40s and Lola T70s to move into the beach buggy business. But John Jobber and Pierre du Plessis of GP Speedshop did just that. In fact, they did it with such success that, like some alien life force, buggies actually took over the whole operation.

In 1967, having discovered a dune buggy called the Lolette while visiting his native South Africa, du Plessis decided to import the moulds into Britain. The resulting GP Beach Buggy was hardly a pretty device, but its bathtub looks and chunky wheels were as far removed from a Ford Cortina MkII as you could get, to the delight of a large minority of young drivers.

The first shell, sold in 1968, cost £140. Customers had to shorten their own Beetle chassis in order to fit it on, but there was no lack of interested parties. GP was soon building complete buggies and taking on plenty of agents to sell them — many of whom later ripped the shell off and sold it under their own names. The boom was on.

Some autocross successes cemented GP's reputation and the firm was not ashamed to tout its wares among the trendy young things of London. At shows, it displayed wild buggies like its purple-and-yellow Velvetex 'Furry Buggy'.

Magazines like *Hot Car* started going buggy barmy; even *Car* magazine, in those less illustrious times, featured a regular column, entitled 'Buggy Off'.

In 1970 GP struggled to keep up as production soared from 10 to 90 kits per month. Pop stars bought them and TV programmes homed in on them. In 1969 GP had introduced a full-length four-seat Super Buggy, which fast became its most popular model. This was followed by the LDV pick-up buggy in 1971 (an estate Ranchero was left until 1974). These were heady days.

They didn't last long. When the summer of '72 arrived, no-one wanted buggies any more. But GP survived the crash for two reasons: its solid reputation as the best of the buggy suppliers and its expansion into export markets (for example, from 1972 on it regularly showed at Geneva). By the end of the 1970s, and despite the collapse of buggydom, sales of GP buggies had reached a phenomenal 3,500.

The firm was lucky not to have to rely on non-buggy products. The Centron of 1970 was intended as a fall-back in case the buggy market proved fruitless but, in the event, just 12 were made in its one-year existence. It did have the distinction of being the UK's first VW Beetle-based exotic kit, with a low glassfibre sports body and a distinctive opening canopy (*à la* Bond Bug). The conventionally-doored MkII Centron (1974) was never properly launched by GP but became one of the most improbable revivals of the 1980s when Lalande relaunched it in 1983. Only two were sold before MDB took it on, equally unsuccessfully, as the Sapphire.

Above: *Yomping over dunes was a rare pleasure for British buggy drivers. Given the chance, the GP Buggy was the one to do it in, as shown on the cover of the February 1970 issue of* Hot Car.

GP's other 1970s offering was the Kubel, a straight replica of the VW Type 181 Kübelwagen on — you guessed it — a Beetle floorpan. Few were sold, although it stumbled on into the 1980s.

The Kubel's creator was Neville Trickett, with whom GP was to storm the next decade with two new models, the Talon and the Madison (for which see Chapter Seven).

Left: *Richard Oakes, stylist of the Nova, went on to become the doyen of kit car designers.*

Nova

Richard Oakes made his design debut in 1970 with the Tramp beach buggy, one of the few originally styled buggies of the British boom. In its year-and-a-half production life, 75 were made.

It was Oakes' next project which put him on the map. The Nova, conceived and styled by Oakes and engineered by Phil Sayers, was completed in December 1971. When launched early the following year, it caused a storm. Nothing quite like it, with the exception of the Lamborghini Miura, had ever been seen before. *Motor* magazine called it 'one of the prettiest cars ever made'. It was available in kit form for just £750, high by kit car standards but still very low by comparison with sports cars of the time.

The centrepiece of the dramatically styled Nova was the lifting canopy which allowed entry to its two occupants. The fact that it was based on the humblest of floorpans, that of the VW Beetle, did not dissuade a healthy line of customers for the car.

Licensed production began in the USA in 1973 with the Sterling. This was the tip of a future iceberg, with modified Nova production starting in France, Italy, Switzerland, Austria, South Africa, and elsewhere.

In Britain, however, the Nova's price told against it during the oil crisis, when car sales slumped overall. In 1975, Automotive Design & Development, the makers of the Nova, went bust, having sold 180 cars. Oakes' fully redesigned Nova replacement never even reached the prototype stage.

Reaction to the Nova had been such that it could not be allowed to die — though the tangled-spaghetti story which followed made some people wish that it had. From 1977, three separate moulds for the Nova began churning out bodyshells from different enterprises, often to a questionable standard of finish. The 'official' version ended up in the hands of Vic Elam in 1978 and the two others joined forces to produce the Nova SSD, which lasted until 1979.

Elam's Nova Cars re-established the exotic, improving it with body mods in 1981 and even mooting a tubular chassis the next year. By 1984, production was running at 12 per month and a Bermuda targa roof version was available.

From this time on, the Nova became more and more of a part-time project. It was eventually sold to new owners in Essex, who are currently still offering the Nova 20 years on.

Volksrod

Warren Monks' Volksrod, completed in Doncaster in 1967, was almost certainly the first British-built beach buggy. The public did not get a taste of it until 1968 when shells for shortened Beetle floorpans went on sale for just £75. By comparison with the fast-selling GP, sales of the Volksrod took a while to get going.

The distinctive slab-sided new Volksrod MkII appeared in 1969 and was joined by a long-wheelbase version a year later. By the time the MkIII swb arrived in August 1970, 270 Volksrods had been made. The MkIV lwb came in 1971.

Sales collapsed in 1972, but Volksrod carried on selling its two models, supported by a general car repair business. Things limped on in ever decreasing circles, but miraculously the Doncaster garage, and recently a new enterprise, managed to continue offering the Volksrod right up to the time of writing.

Above: *Completed in December 1971, the Nova mated an exotic GRP body with nothing more adventurous than a VW chassis.*

Right: *This was Britain's first beach buggy, the Volksrod.*

Manta Ray

One of the first entrepreneurs to realise that you could rip off a buggy shell and sell it as your own was Adrian Harrington, who did it with a GP shell in 1969. The Harrington & King's Sports Buggy was a bit of a mouthful, but was cheap at £105.

The company ripped off an American design next, launching the Manta Ray in late 1969. With its swooping lines and frogeye headlamps, the Manta Ray at least looked different. Despite appalling quality, almost 200 were sold before the firm's demise towards the end of 1971.

Revived in 1972, the Manta Ray became just another tired old buggy. The last one was made in 1980, although there was a baffling revival in 1986, followed by a last-ditch stand with GT Mouldings.

Rat

Yet another example of plastic surgery on a GP shell, the Rat was quite heavily modified to distinguish it from its predecessor. Made by Fibre-Fab from 1970, it became one of the more popular second-string buggies and remained in production until 1981, when production was up to 400.

Taken over by Tim Cooksey, who renamed the firm FF, the Rat underwent numerous changes to make it more sophisticated, culminating in FF's own Buggy. By the late 1980s its attractions had faded, though it was revived by Country Volks from 1987 on.

Dutton

Tim Dutton-Woolley was clever enough, or lucky enough, to hit upon a winning formula when he built his P1 in 1970. He saw that there were no cheap Lotus Seven-style cars on the market, so that was what he created. And that was what made him progressively the biggest kit manufacturer in Britain, then Europe, then the world.

The P1 design was simple: a spaceframe chassis with aluminium body panels plus Lotus Seven wings and a GRP nosecone, and Austin-Healey Sprite mechanicals. Nine were built in a year.

The need for a less collectable base vehicle led to the Dutton B-Type of 1971. Of similar layout, it used Herald front suspension and Herald or Spitfire engines, with BMC, Ford and Alfa Romeo units optional. The bodywork was now mostly GRP. Basic kits sold for as little as £220, although Dutton did offer complete kits with all-new Ford parts for which there were few takers.

Weighing only 9.5cwt, the B-Type was nimble and handled well, but suffered from a spine-jarring ride and spartan interior. In 1973, the slightly more refined B-Plus was launched alongside the B-Type (which lasted until 1974, when 250 had been sold). The B-Plus had a more substantial chassis designed to accept a Ford Cortina rear axle and larger engines. The body was larger, too, and could be distinguished by its wings, which now lacked sidelights.

The Malaga was planned for 1973 but was delayed until 1975. It was simply a different body option, featuring curved front wings and a sloping rear end, although the front and rear of both models were interchangeable. The most powerful engine option was the 138bhp Ford three-litre V6, tested from 0 to 60mph in 6.4 seconds.

The 500th Dutton was made in May 1977 as production levels continued to rise, defying the slump in the rest of the kit car industry. By the time both Dutton's models were replaced in 1978, about 450 of each had been sold.

An unusual departure for Dutton was the Cantera of 1976. A modified B-Plus chassis sat under a two-seater GRP body of odd proportions and angular profile. Again, its ride was the closest the motor industry had come to sledging over potholes and its price (£475) attracted just 11 orders before it died in 1977.

Dutton's most important model, the Phaeton, was announced prematurely in 1976. By 1977, it was sporting a Polski-Fiat engine as negotiations went on for a production run in Poland... The production Phaeton finally arrived in 1978, offering a rationalised spec using mostly Ford components in a lengthened chassis. Priced at £406, 200 were sold in its first six months of production: the Phaeton was Europe's fastest-selling kit, averaging about seven per week. Revised throughout the 1980s, it remained Dutton's mainstay until the end.

Dutton entered the 1980s, its most triumphant period, with another model, the Sierra, launched at the 1979 Motorfair. For the remaining instalment of the Dutton chronicles, see Chapter Seven.

***Right:** One of the few buggies which tried to look a bit different from the GP was the Manta Ray. Ironically, it was financed by the sales of a copy of the GP shell.*

***Below:** Perhaps it was this buggy's low nose which inspired its name — the Rat.*

***Right:** This was the car which founded a dynasty. The Dutton B-Plus had all the right elements: minimalist body, simple construction and a very low price. 450 were sold.*

Siva

Neville Trickett has been one of the very few British designers to remain consistently active over three decades, from the 1960s to the 1990s. His 'middle period' was by far his most prolific.

Having successfully put the Opus HRF into production in 1966, Trickett formed Neville Trickett (Design) Ltd a year later to design a succession of bizarre vehicles including two different Bentley MkVI shells. Mike Saunders, who ran a firm called Siva Engineering, approached Trickett with a plan for creating an Edwardian-style glassfibre body on a Ford Popular E93A chassis.

Launched in 1969, the Siva Edwardian involved Trickett to perhaps a greater extent than he had intended: he not only designed it, but manufactured it, too. Sold as a kit for just £125, or complete for £355, its humour was not lost on the buying public. Called the Edwardian Roadster, the two-seater car was quickly followed by the four-seater Tourer. By 1974 a total of 105 Edwardians had been sold. 80 of them were tourers — an achievement at least partly attributable to the fact that Jon Pertwee had driven one in the popular BBC television series, *Dr Who*.

The impertinence of the thing was multiplied in Trickett's Raceabout of 1970. Still looking like the property of some moustache-twitching aristocrat in an earlier age, the two-seater body was plonked on top of a VW Beetle chassis. Among the options listed were a monocle windscreen and 18in artillery wheels. Its utter impracticality — no weather equipment was ever offered — was probably the reason why sales by 1975 had totalled no more than six.

In 1970, being a great fan of Citroen's 2CV, Trickett decided to alter a Tourer body to fit the chassis of the famous little car. He called it the Parisienne. Buyers were at least protected against the weather but, on the other hand, were unable to travel faster than 50mph. British customers were not really ready for a 2CV-based kit and bought only seven before the model's demise in 1975.

1970 was an industrious twelve months for Trickett, as the four-seater version of the VW-based Raceabout also appeared that year. Trickett named it the San Remo, but the exotic name did nothing for sales: just eight were made.

There were further shenanigans that year when Trickett launched two Mini-based kits. The first was the Siva Mule, a sort of Moke-style jeep which mated a tubular chassis, a GRP body and Mini subframes in a practical four-seater vehicle. Its 13-inch wheels made it useful off-road, but between its debut and its demise in 1975 only 12 were produced.

The Siva Mini Buggy hardly fared better. This was a classically-styled beach buggy, which ambitiously used Mini subframes in a kit more expensive than most VW buggies.

It is almost unbelievable that Trickett also completed yet another car that year. Its origins lay in an Imp-based GT coupé commissioned by Marcos in 1969 but dropped by them. Trickett just managed to get the car finished for its January 1971 debut, when it was presented as the Siva Spyder — in open form because its gullwing doors weren't ready. One Spyder was actually sold before the gullwing version, the S160, was launched soon afterwards. Based on a VW Beetle floorpan, the very complete kit cost £895 — quite a lot of money, by kit car standards — and just 12 S160s were sold. The S530 development was sold only in complete form (see Chapter Six).

Its replacement was the Saluki of 1973. A very mature design, its futuristic lines belied its Beetle basis: pop-up headlamps, gullwing doors and a curious box-like instrument binnacle were its features. Poorly marketed, like all Siva products, it sold a disappointing 50 examples by 1976. Mike Carlton of Embeesea then modified it as the Chepeko and, later, the Charger (see Chapter Seven).

In 1972 Trickett built the Siva Llama, based on Mule body panels but using Hillman Imp mechanicals. Intended to be sold complete in the UK and in complete knock-down form for third world countries, it called for a host of minor changes which delayed its launch until 1974. Its best feature was the interchangeability of its body, from jeep to pick-up to van.

Despite promising interest, the Llama shared the fate of all Sivas: dreadful sales. Only 50 or so were made before Siva went under in 1976. Dragged down at the same time were the Sierra, a new jeep-type utility car based on the Escort 1300, of which three were made, and a replica of the Citroen Mehari 'jeep'.

Trickett survived the ignominy to go on to manufacture hovercraft and his Kubel for GP, with whom he developed a fruitful liaison in the 1980s: see Chapter Seven.

Right: *The Siva marque blossomed from the pen of designer Neville Trickett (seen driving his Mule, to the rear). The Beetle-based Raceabout, in front, was either a great laugh or a damned impertinence, depending on where one's sympathies lay.*

Below: *Trickett's Siva Saluki was a dramatic gullwing coupé.*

Left: *The MkI Mini-Scamp made no bones about its basic appeal.*

Opposite page
There was no doubting the chassis strength of the Jago Sandero, which began life with the name Geep.

Mini-Scamp

Robert Mandry's idea of a Mini-Moke replacement was the first of the many. The Mini-Scamp was born in 1970, a very squarish open jeep using Mini subframes and components in a tubular chassis clothed with all-metal panels. Cheap at £175 for the kit, it appealed both to the city trendies who had lost the Moke (production had been transferred to Australia) and to those whose interest lay in pressing it into rougher duties.

The versatility of the design quickly became apparent and all manner of strange Scamps started being made. There were hard-tops and soft-tops, a long-wheelbase six-seater used for picking up parachute jumpers, an ultra-short-wheelbase two-seater, six-wheelers — just about any body-size or format could be ordered. Pretty soon, the tough little Mini-Scamp had friends all over the world and was selling handsomely. Production of MkI Scamps reached 700.

Mandy decided that the concept needed updating and launched the MkII in 1978. This was different in almost all respects from the earlier car, sharing only its mechanical specification. The body was still aluminium, but had a new square nose and the option of a gullwing hardtop. Kits cost £465 and the new version became even more popular than its predecessor.

By the mid-1980s, Mandy had lost interest in the Scamp and ceased to advertise it. He sold the project in 1987 to the Scamp Motor Co of East Grinstead, who revived it and improved on the chassis design. A restyled MkIII version appeared in 1990 and remains available today in just as many forms as the original. About 3,000 Scamps have so far been made.

Jago

Geoff Jago was the man responsible for the first British hot rod kit in 1965, and he sold hundreds of them. Perhaps realising that demand for such outlandish contraptions might not last, he diversified by building up a chassis manufacturing service (customers even included Panther Westwinds) and a range of kit cars.

Jago's first kit was the Jeep of 1971. This was a pretty close replica of the Willys Jeep — not surprising, as its body was moulded from an original Jeep. Based on a simple ladder chassis containing nothing more rough-and-tumble than Ford Anglia 105E components, it was cheap at £190 for the kit and even offered a hood and sidescreens.

Its favourable reception did not impress American Motors, who demanded that the name be changed. Jago duly changed it — to Geep! He also offered a Morris Minor-based version in 1974, but the definitive Escort-based Geep did not arrive until 1976, by which time several hundred kits had been made. Many were used off-road.

The Geep saw many refinements over the following years, including a roll-cage in 1984 and completely revised bodywork in 1987. It remained a consistent seller throughout the decade. In 1991, in an agreement with Chrysler, the car was again renamed to become the Sandero.

This was a name first used on a prototype Jago estate/pick-up of 1983, which never saw production. Also that year came the Samuri, a sort of civilised Ford-engined four-seater buggy with a hard-top. Its practicalities did not go unnoticed, but the supply of customers was quickly exhausted and the Samuri was dropped in 1990.

HOW 805X

AF

Alexander Fraser's little Mini-based three-wheelers took their inspiration from the Morgans of which Fraser was a great enthusiast. Built together with Colin Crabbe in 1971, his first car, the AB1, had a marine plywood body/chassis mated to a Mini front subframe, with a steel frame supporting a single Mini trailing arm at the rear. Kits were offered at £275, but there was hardly a chance to buy one before Fraser's updated model, the AF Spider, arrived later the same year.

This had a similar point-tailed body and layout to the AB1. *Motor* magazine drove one and commented that it resembled a mobile wardrobe, though the tester did describe the experience as the most fun he had had in ten years. Weighing just 952lbs, it was quick: one with a tuned engine reached 60mph from rest in 8.7 seconds! But it suffered from severe understeer.

Very few were made before the firm wound up in 1972. Fraser then redesigned the car with cycle wings and a rounded rear end, calling it the Grand Prix. From his workshop in Marlborough he went on to build four of them to special order, the last one in 1980.

Below: *The most desirable of Mini-based three-wheeler was the quirky AF Spider of 1971, the sort of car which inspires schoolboys to ask how fast it will go in water.*

Bottom: *Smoother AF Grand Prix had a rounded rear end.*

Stimson

Alongside Neville Trickett, Barrie Stimson stands pre-eminent as one of the all-time mad-hatters of British car design. His prodigious output of increasingly off-beat conveyances in the 1970s tottered along the fine line between genius and madness.

His topsy-turvy career began in 1970, with the building of the prototype Mini Bug, constructed in one week on a budget of £25. Using a spaceframe chassis into which Mini bits fitted, the Mini Bug, with its GRP buggy body, was to say the least unusual. The head-lamps sat just in front of the windscreen, the offside surround of which was moulded from a brassiere...

At £170, the kit started to sell, spurred by its twin claims to fame as 'the first ever Mini-Based buggy' and 'the ugliest car around'. By late 1970, Stimson had built 20 of them.

Its replacement, the Mini Bug 2, arrived early in 1971 with more rounded lines, a one-piece lift-off front end and a GRP targa bar. It was a more respectable but still whacky version which weighed just 9cwt and shared the earlier car's handling and performance. Even a CS+I racer with a triangular spaceframe chassis was built, but it was bought by only four people compared with sales of 160 for the Mini Bug 2.

Stimson's Safari Six of 1972 was an attractive and practical six-wheeled pick-up, again on Mini bits. Available with full weather equipment, it promised much; but the ambitious plans for it led to financial wranglings — an area where Stimson never felt at ease — and in 1973 he folded the company with only about 20 sold. The planned four-wheeled Safari Four never became a reality. Automotive Services bought the rights to the Safari Six and developed it with Peugeot and Fiesta power, intending to launch the car, renamed the Shikari, as a fully-built vehicle. Nothing ever came of it.

Stimson lived abroad for a while, but on his return attacked the CS+I project again, launching a road version, the CS+II, in 1976. It differed only in detail from the Mini Bug 2 (including a roll-cage). Just two CS+IIs were sold before a new firm, Mini Motors of Rochdale, took it over in 1977 and changed its name to CS2 in 1979. They sold over 40 cars before the Bug again changed hands in 1982. Confusingly renamed the CS+2, an electric version was also offered; but by now the whole project was on its last legs and, by 1986, it had simply faded away.

Right: *Attractive six-wheeled Mini-based Stimson Safari Six was a rather restrained effort from Barrie Stimson's pen.*

Below, right: *Stimson CS+II, 1976: a fun car based on Stimson's earlier Mini Bug series.*

Meanwhile, Stimson was concentrating on another bizarre idea: the Scorcher, of 1976. This contraption was a three-wheeler using a Mini front subframe in a triangulated tubular chassis, over which was fitted a curious GRP body. The driver and his two passengers sat astride the Scorcher as if on horseback, mercilessly exposed to the elements. The tax authorities had trouble labelling it and eventually classed it as a motorcycle and sidecar! Weight was just 5cwt and phenomenal performance was possible.

By 1981, after only 30 had been made, Stimson tired of the Scorcher, sold it on and, later that year, introduced his final UK project. The Trek, as it was called, was a tall Mini-based fun car, a three-seater again, with a familiar arrangement whereby the driver straddled a central tunnel and the two passengers sat either side of it behind him. £924 was the kit's asking price.

Mediocre sales, and an artist's disenchantment with life in Britain, led Stimson to emigrate to France. He sold the Trek to a firm called Sarronset, which lasted only two years.

Other Stimson projects had included the C-Donki, a dinghy which could be driven on stilts when on dry land, and a Honda Acty-based leisure vehicle. When the author last spoke to him, Stimson was musing on the possibility of creating a 40-foot high pink plastic pig in glassfibre. 'People would pay to walk in through the mouth and leave by its arsehole,' he said. Where are you now, Barrie?

Above, right: *Whacky Stimson Scorcher defied categorisation.*

Right: *Stimson's final fling: the Trek three-seater of 1981.*

Above: *Davrians new and old. The Mk8 (left) was their last model.*

Davrian

Adrian Evans' Davrian began life in prototype form in 1965 as a curvaceous open two-seater based on Hillman Imp parts. Its GRP monocoque construction was light and strong. A few open cars were sold from 1967, but it was the enclosed coupé Demon (1968) which became the Davrian standard.

Many customers saw in the Davrian a cheap way into race and rally driving, something Evans actively pushed. Davrians started notching up competition wins, culminating in a victory in Modsports in 1974. By 1972, 200 had been built.

As the range of engines available expanded to include Mini, Ford and VW, the Davrian progressed through a number of Mks, up to the Mk8 of 1980. By now, having moved from London to Lampeter in 1976, Davrian was considered a Welsh marque. The up-market Fiesta-powered version of the Mk8, which sold for a whopping £5,322, was designated the Dragon.

Over-extended, Davrian went under in 1983. Corry Cars took it over and developed the rather different, but disastrous, Cultra. Finally the project came to rest with Lampeter-based Team Duffee Engineering, where at time of writing a modified version, known as the Darrian T9, is still available.

Magenta

Glassfibre specialists Lightspeed Panels produced their own fun car, the Magenta, in 1972. Unusually, it used the BMC1100/1300 as its basis (even the grille came from an MG 1100), and its GRP body was distinctive, if somewhat awkward. Still, you got a strong and well-handling car, 2+2 accommodation and the option of a hardtop.

The Magenta became a most improbable rallying success in the 1970s; one example even competed in the 1977 London-Sydney event. Magentas sold in their hundreds. Lightspeed Panels also marketed Cartune's Apal buggy as late as 1975.

The Escort-based Magenta LSR appeared in 1978, going into production a year later and followed in 1980 by the Mini-based Sprint. Both had minor bodywork differences. In 1982, the all-new Escort-based Tarragon 'sportshatch' arrived; an improved version, the TXR, was equally uncomfortable. In 1986, when Magenta went bust, there were few who mourned.

Futura

The name of Robin Statham is unlikely to ring any bells, but had his Futura ever made it into proper production, it would surely still be well-known.

Statham was the proprietor of Jem Cars, manufacturers of the successful little Minijem. He embarked on his ambitious GT project in 1970 and showed a completed mock-up at the 1971 Racing Car Show.

The Futura was a stunning design, a low wedge whose most striking feature was its mode of entry: a side-hingeing windscreen allowing access over the car's front edge. The prototype's four headlamps arranged behind the windscreen would have been illegal, so pop-up units were planned. The fact that it was all on a Beetle floorpan (a fact for which the brochure apologised!) hardly seemed to matter.

But the cost of developing the Futura broke the company in July 1971, taking the Minijem with it. Only three bodyshells had been made, one of which, in pieces, found its way to Brazil.

Above: *Despite the ungainliness of its lines, the Magenta was a strong seller. This is the LSR of 1978.*

Below: *1971 Futura. The only way in was by lifting up the windscreen and stepping over the front of the car.*

TX Tripper

Of no other car can it be claimed that it was born as the result of a stomach ulcer. Torix Bennett, son of the founder of Fairthorpe, was languishing in hospital musing on the difficulties of producing the Fairthorpe TX-GT when, in a flash of inspiration, he beheld in his mind's eye the form of the Tripper — a car which would be beautifully easy to manufacture.

But the Tripper was anything but beautiful to behold. A collision of contorted curves, obscene bulges and 'wobbly bits', it was a kind of buggy/sports car cross-over which used a Triumph Spitfire chassis.

Unleashed at the 1971 Racing Car Show, the TX Tripper raised a few eyebrows, but also a few wallet-flaps at a price of £180 or £740 complete. Originally the Tripper had rearward-facing rear seats, but the daftness of this idea obviously dawned on Bennett as they were soon changed to face in the expected direction. He also realised halfway through 1971 that a Triumph 2.5 Pi engine would squeeze under the bonnet and, by deduction, a 152bhp TR6. A demonstrator with this engine in place became a celebrated press car, recording figures of 125mph and 0-60mph in 6.4 seconds!

With the introduction of a hard-top and a lockable boot, the Tripper was surely getting too close to normality for comfort. About 60 were sold before the crippling effects of VAT forced production down — only two were built in 1974 — and Bennett was obliged to make bathtubs without wheels to pay his way. By 1979, when he finally withdrew the Tripper from sale, production totalled about 80. Only one was exported, though more might have gone to Switzerland had not a Swiss doctor pointed out that in his home territory Tripper translated as 'gonorrhea'.

The Tripper was twice revived, in 1983 and 1986, though with no more success than one would imagine. It is better to remember the Tripper as a symbol of those carefree and wobblesome days of the psychedelic fun car.

Voodoo

Surely one of the prettiest kit cars ever made was the Voodoo. Its tragedy, as with so many exotic kit car projects, was that it never made it into production.

To start with, in fact, it was not even intended to enter production. John Arnold, its designer, and Geoff Neale planned to build just two Voodoos, one for each of them. However, when the prototype appeared at the 1971 Motor Show, a third party stepped in with the offer of financial backing for a production run.

Based around a spaceframe chassis, the Voodoo used an Imp Sport engine clothed in a dramatic but tasteful GRP body only 35 inches high. Entry was by raising a gas-assisted canopy. Weighing just 11cwt, it was an excellent performer (115mph) and, at an expected price of £2,000 for a very complete car, the omens were promising.

Opposite page
The TX Tripper was a quite bizarre contraption, styled by ex-Fairthorpe man Torix Bennett.

This page
Right: *Had it entered production, the Voodoo would surely be recognised as a styling great. Just three were made.*

Below: *1973 Piper P2: a well-conceived and striking sports coupé.*

That old black magic intervened in 1973, first when the financier pulled out (where have we heard that before?) and again when John Arnold was tragically killed in a car crash. A third Voodoo was under construction at the time.

Geoff Neale planned a revival in the early 1980s, but insufficient interest was shown and the Voodoo remained in its grave.

Piper

Ex-Brabham, McLaren and Lola man Tony Hilder designed the beautiful open Piper GT, launched in 1967. It was offered with Ford 1600GT, Hillman Imp and BMC A-series engines (the last subsequently known as the GTA) and kits were put on sale at £399. Only six were made before build-up problems halted production.

The project was relaunched by Brian Sherwood in 1968 as the GTT, now in closed form. A Ford 1600 engine now fitted into the steel backbone chassis. Much praise was showered on its handsomely curved and sleek coupe glassfibre bodywork.

By 1969, it had been joined by a gullwing GTT, a luxury version called the GTS, and the GTR, a stunning Group Six racing prototype, of which only four were made. A later plan to market it as a VW-based road car never came off, perhaps fortunately.

Sherwood's death at the wheel of a Piper shook the operation, but it continued through 1970 with a peak production-rate of two cars per month. The following year, the lengthened P2 (Phase 2) replaced the GTT, of which 50 had been built. The P2 had a stronger chassis, improved rear suspension and a longer nose with circular headlamps. But strikes at Ford led to engine supply problems and Piper went bust in June 1971.

Production restarted in 1972, the P2 now with pop-up headlamps and a Ford 2-litre engine. With the introduction of VAT in 1973, Piper stopped selling kit-form cars; a complete P2 now cost nearly £2,000. By this time, the Piper was a well-respected hand-built sports car. But sales slowed dramatically and production ceased late in 1974 with about 150 cars completed. Piper itself continues today, well-known for its camshafts.

TiCi

Furniture design lecturer Anthony Hill's first study in town car design was a 500cc Triumph Daytona-engined prototype in 1969. When the fun car boom arrived, Hill seized the opportunity to put an enlarged version into production.

The new TiCi (pronounced 'titchy') was very, very short — 89 inches — and used a Mini front subframe mounted behind the two passengers in an arrangement optimistically described as 'mid-engined'. Its GRP monocoque body was an eccentric box shape; in yellow livery, as all TiCis came, it was known affectionately by some as 'the skip'.

Described as a 'city sprint commuter car', it got the backing of Stirling Moss and financial support from ex-BRM sponsor Raymond Mays. Kits became available in 1972 at a price of £395, with a hard top and doors optional at £35. But, like so many other 1970s funsters, VAT killed it in 1974, after only a measly 40 had been made. A notable owner was Clive Sinclair, who made an electric version...

The author owned the prototype briefly and can report that it went quite fast, despite its 848cc Minivan engine, and was immense fun. It was, however, one of the most impractical cars he has ever driven. A London cabbie pulled up alongside him in traffic one day and asked what he had done with the other roller-skate. Ho ho.

Spartan

Along with the RMB Gentry, the Spartan was just about the only retro-style kit of the 1970s. Both shared similar specifications and an enormous popularity. Indeed, it is amazing that no-one else jumped on the bandwagon sooner.

The Spartan was the 1972 brainchild of Jim McIntyre and was an obviously MG-inspired design based on a Triumph Herald, Vitesse or Spitfire chassis. Bodywork was in aluminium with GRP wings and the initial cars had 'suicide' doors, which were soon changed. The kit price was £275 and Spartan were soon enjoying healthy sales. For much of the 1970s, in fact, it was Britain's most successful kit car firm, beating even Dutton. By 1977, 500 had been sold.

Its own chassis arrived in 1974 and was followed, a year later, by the 2+2. As the years progressed, Ford engines became the standard choice for Spartans. Despite McIntyre distancing himself from the kit car scene, Spartans continued to sell well: they are still available at time of writing and it is claimed that the total built exceeds 4,000.

Top: *Clever, impractical, and fun: the 'city sprint commuter' TiCi.*

Below: *One of the great successes of the 1970s: The MG-inspired Spartan.*

Ranger

The Ranger was one of the most successful cars of the fun kit boom, and one of the few which actually outlasted it. It arrived in late 1971 when enthusiasm was at its highest, its attractions based on its chunky jeep styling and BMC 1100/1300 chassis.

Priced competitively at £245, the GRP body/chassis kit sold in large numbers, helped by a good soft-top and the option of a hard-top. Several hundred were sold within only three years; but in 1974 they dropped sharply and Ranger might have gone to the wall but for the good response to its second model, the Cub.

A three-wheeler on Mini parts might sound an unlikely candidate for sales success, but as soon as the Cub was launched in 1974 its cheeky styling brought in orders at the rate of three per week. Handling was surprisingly good and, with its optional boot and hood fitted, the Cub was practical too.

Even so, by 1976 Ranger was struggling and in April that year production of both its models came to a halt. About 200 Cubs had been made, including four with four wheels and pick-up rear bodywork. There was even an electric Cub. A six-wheeled version of the original Ranger remained a prototype only.

In 1984, the Ranger jeep was revived in modified form by a firm in Wales. Called the Ranger 80, it hardly lasted one season.

Top: *1974 Ranger Cub: Mini-based three-wheeled two-seater.*
Above: *The four-wheeled version of the Ranger Cub had a large pick-up area, but it never got much of a chance to show its mettle.*

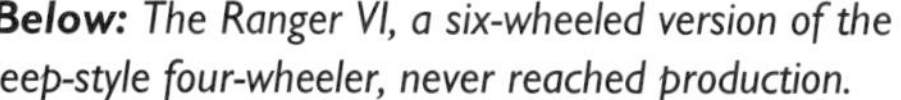

Below: *The Ranger VI, a six-wheeled version of the jeep-style four-wheeler, never reached production.*

Left: *The Status Minipower, of which Colin Chapman is reputed to have said, 'This is how the Lotus Seven S4 should have been'.*

Below: *The Status 365 was styled by Lotus Elite stylist John Frayling. One can see a distant similarity.*

Status

Brian Luff left Lotus as vehicle engineering manager in 1970 and immediately formed Status Cars to sell the Mini-based spaceframe chassis he had designed. His freelance specialist work also included the engineering elements of the Clan Crusader and the revision of the Gilbern Invader.

But it was Status which was Luff's consuming passion. Instead of offering just a chassis (mostly to DIY autocross drivers), he set about creating an open glassfibre body for it. Born of his dissatisfaction with the Lotus Seven S4, which he said had 'deteriorated into a crumpet catcher', the car was completed in 1971, named the Status Symbol.

The car's great strength was its excellent chassis, which bore resemblances to Formula One design, down to the gearstick mounted to the right of the driver. Double wishbone suspension was fitted front and rear. Any BMC A-series engine could be installed behind the passengers, driving through BMC 1100 driveshafts. It weighed only 9cwt and performance, whichever unit was fitted, was superb.

Pure road Symbols began production in 1972 (the name changed to Minipower soon after). A hardtop supplemented the soft-top option within months. But the Minipower simply proved uneconomic to produce and, after 20 chassis had been made, production stopped in 1973. Just eight bodies had been supplied for road cars.

Luff survived, making fake Rolls-Royce grilles for Minis and Clan bodyshells. His next kit car project was the Status 365, so called because it was designed to be practical all year round. Launched in 1974, it used Mini subframes in a GRP-and-wood monocoque body unit of rather odd angular design. Distinguishing points were four seats and curious three-piece front windows.

Despite its practicality, only about 40 were made, although in theory it remained available until the early 1980s. Luff went on to develop the Mini Minus of 1982, but it was productionised by Minus Cars. In 1991, he relaunched the Status marque with the Mini-based Sabot sports car.

Above: *Gullwing Charger was developed from the Siva Saluki.*

Charger

After Neville Trickett's Siva Saluki passed out of his hands, a modified example was launched in 1975 by Mike Carlton's Embeesea Kit Cars. Designated the Chepeko, it had a shorter rear end and revised frontal treatment (minus pop-up headlamps). Whether these revisions made it look any prettier was a matter of opinion.

Very few were made before it was replaced in 1977 by the restyled but still Beetle-based Charger, now with a front spoiler and larger versions of the gullwing doors. The Charger looked like being charged out by Embeesea's Eurocco of 1979 (for which involved story see Chapter Seven), but it wasn't.

Indeed, it was joined in 1983 by the Charger 2, a 2+2 version which unfortunately looked even less lovely than the Charger 1, which effectively bowed out at the same time. Further on that year, the firm's name changed to the MBC Car Company, but only a year later it ducked out and DJ Sportscars took over Chargers 1 and 2.

By 1986, they had passed on to MDB Sportscars, which marketed them briefly under the mysterious names Saratoga and Saturn respectively. MDB did not last long enough to introduce its Cortina-based chassis. A Welsh firm called Viking offered the models as the Dragonfire and Dragonfly briefly in 1987. End of story, with several hundred Chargers, and rather fewer Charger 2s, sold.

Above: *1979 Pelland Sports: extremely low and rakish roadster which used a mid-mounted VW or Ford engine.*

Pelland Sports

Peter Pellandine had left Britain for Australia back in 1962, abandoning his Falcon marque (see Chapter Two). During the 1970s, he began designing and building two sports designs under the name Pellandini. He returned to Britain in 1978 and the following year began offering the second of his Australian kits on the UK market, which he called the Pelland Sports.

This was a very low (35-inch) doorless two-seater of monocoque GRP construction. Its engine, either a VW Beetle or a four-cylinder Ford, was mounted back-to-front ahead of the transaxle, making it a mid-engined car. Handling was superb, thanks to specially designed leaf rear suspension, and, with a weight of just 9cwt, so was performance. A hard top, with removable mini-gullwings to allow entry, was an optional extra.

Only a year later, in 1980, Pellandine sold the project to Ryder Designs — who marketed it as the Ryder Rembrandt — and concentrated on the steam-powered car in which he hoped to break the world steam-powered speed record. This project had begun as early as 1976, with support from the Australian government. But bugs beleaguered his efforts right up to the latest, unsuccessful attempt in 1991.

The original Pelland Sports, meanwhile, passed from Ryder to Graham Autos in 1982, then to Listair, where it was restyled and renamed the Dash. Eventually it came to Dash sportscars, by which time it had Alfasud power. At time of writing, it is still available.

Chapter Six

Coachbuilt Cars of the 1970s

A fly transported back in time to the beginning of the 1970s would find itself caught in a collective buzz of euphoria. The experimentation evident in music, design, dress and other aspects of British culture was bursting through in car design too.

The early 1970s promised much. A host of exotic concept cars was following hot on the trail of the tremendously exciting Lamborghini Miura. Britain's Dennis Adams made worldwide headlines with his Design Probe series, spectacularly low and rakish cars whose like had never been seen.

It became apparent that there was a good market for expensive automotive playthings. Many companies thrived on the desire for brave new creations, offering weird and wonderful machines more for fun than practicality: from the outlandish Bond Bug to the Guyson E12, the seeds of a broadening design horizon bore strange new fruit.

Another uniquely 1970s phenomenon was the 'replicar'. The idea of making cars which looked as though they came from a different era but actually hid up-to-date mechanicals underneath originated in (where else?) America: the first successful replicar (or 'neo-classic', in American parlance) was the Excalibur of 1966.

Many British firms took up the idea. The first was the Albany, a thoroughly convincing Edwardian-style device of 1971, described by its makers as 'a veteran for everyday use'.

A retro-style design also launched the most colourful specialist maker of the 1970s: Panther. The J72 became very chic as a dashingly expensive toy favoured by film and rock stars. It allowed Robert Jankel, Panther's mentor, the freedom to create a startling succession of bizarre, opulent, often vulgar vehicles. Panther's most famous model, the Lima, was a shamelessly sham 'thirties-ish sports car.

The replicar idea really took off with painstakingly original copies of all sorts of classics, such as the Jaguar C and D Type, Healey Le Mans and Bugatti Type 35. One example of the last was allowed out with the intriguing name of Dri-Sleeve Moonraker! There were also numerous attempts to design cars which, while not replicas, were deliberately reminiscent of the styling themes of the 1930s. These included the Mallalieu, Johnard and Syd Lawrence cars, based around Bentley Mk6 mechanicals.

The 1970s ushered in a wave of bold new designers who managed to get their cars most, or all, of the way to production. Neville Trickett successfully established his Siva marque; William Towns took the Guyson and GS Europa into production; Chris Humberstone made many prototypes on the way to getting Rapport started; Chris Lawrence brought about the promising but ill-fated Monica; and Tony Stevens designed the beautiful little Cipher.

Some of the bigger specialist firms began to look outwards, too, with styling exercises and commissioned one-offs. Aston Martin dabbled with the Ogle 'Sotheby Special' (1972) and the Bulldog (1978), while TVR tried the unusual-looking SM, or Zanté (1971).

But as quickly as the enthusiasm of the early 1970s brought proliferation, so the combined effects of the 1973 oil crisis, the introduction of Value Added Tax and an economy facing decline led to a wholesale collapse of Britain's specialist car industry.

It was not just the small names which fluttered out, but the famous ones too. The graveyard of the mid-1970s included Jensen, Aston Martin, Gilbern, Clan, Bond, Trident and Fairthorpe. Ginetta and AC tottered precariously for most of the rest of the decade. Marcos had already hit the wall in 1971. Even Panther failed to survive the decade, ducking out in 1979 (though it was later rescued by Korean tycoon Young C. Kim).

In fact, out of the entire roll-call of minor manufacturers in the 1970s, only two firms survived intact to face the succeeding decade. Caterham Cars, having taken over production of the Lotus 7 in 1973, actually flourished, shrewdly opting to make the Series 3 Super Seven last made by Lotus in 1969 instead of the unpopular Series 4. And Ginetta, which held on tenuously to life with the very low-volume G21, effectively returned to kit car manufacture in the 1980s as the only way to survive.

From near-unbridled optimism, in fact, the 1970s turned into a decade of nightmarish uncertainty for the specialist industry. Yet despite the turbulent economic waters in which most companies sank, some of the liveliest and most interesting designs were produced during the decade, providing a much-needed antedote to the increasingly dull and mediocre offerings of the large-scale firms.

Opposite page
Clan Crusaders are finished at Clan's 23,000-sq ft factory in Washington, County Durham, in 1971.

Clan

The Clan Crusader was a courageous bid by a breakaway group of ex-Lotus engineers to exploit a sub-Elan sports car market. Headed by Paul Haussauer (the original project engineer on the second-generation Lotus Elite), the team included Brian Luff (later of Status Cars) and John Frayling (designer of the Lotus Europa) who styled the car.

A rare attempt at a virtually all-glassfibre monocoque design, the Clan was low and sleek, with a Cd of 0.32. Like the Ginetta G15 — very much its rival — it used the 51bhp Sunbeam Stiletto 875cc engine which powered it to 100mph. It wasn't cheap when it debuted in 1971 — £1,339 complete or £1,125 as a kit — but it won many friends. However, the world economic crisis put paid to the project by Christmas 1973. Including unfinished cars, production totalled 325.

The project was sold to a Cypriot who carried out some development on the car but took matters no further than that. And there have been other attempts to revive the Clan. Brian Luff offered Clan shells for some time through his company Status, then sold the moulds to an enthusiast who made 12 more kits by 1982. Paul Haussauer himself tried once more in the 1980s, but his efforts were again fruitless. More successful were the restyled Clan from Northern Ireland and the Clan-inspired McCoy of the 1980s.

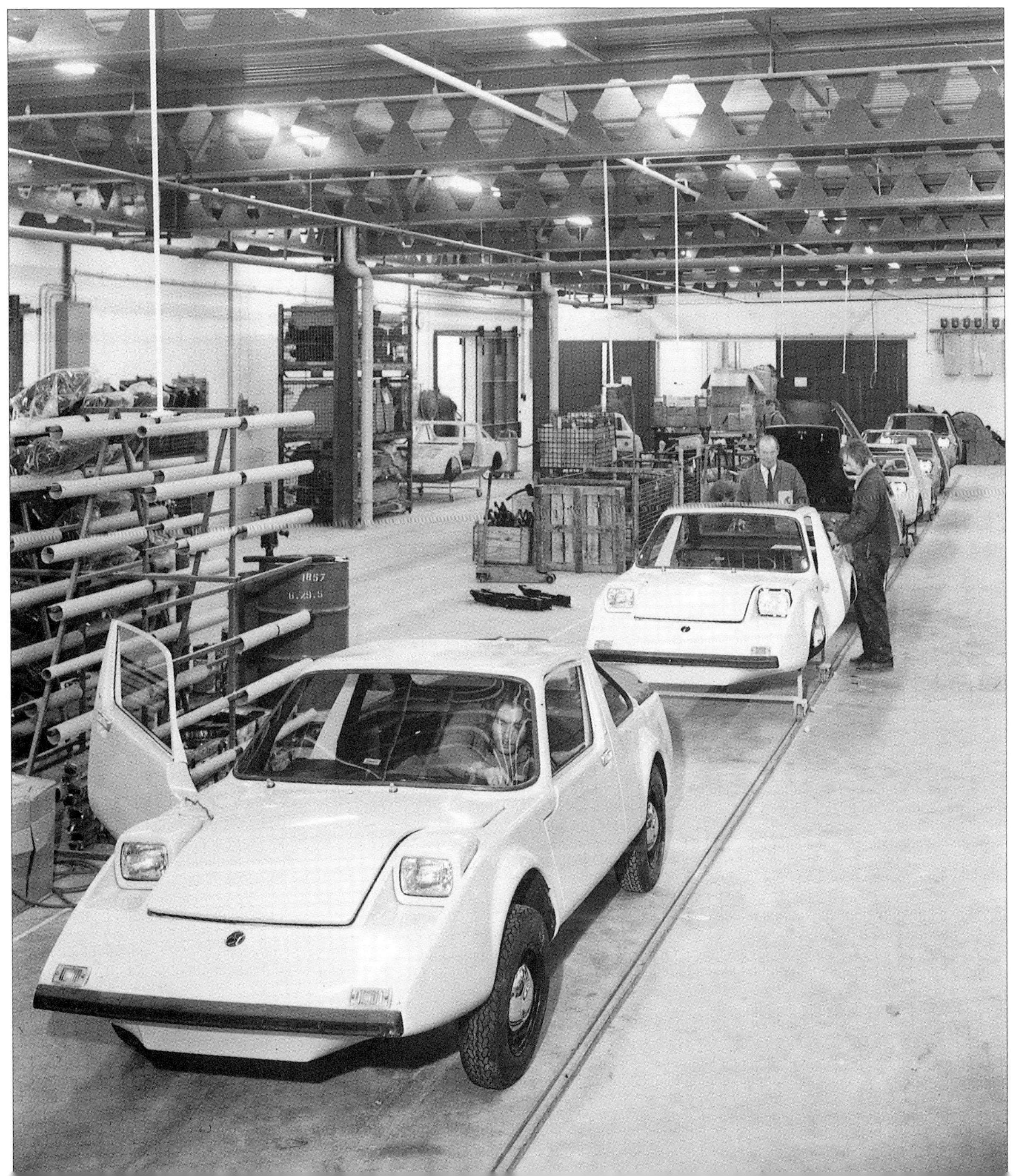

Clan

Met Way
Met Way
EXIT
ALLARD GOLDE
SUN ROOFS
by
ALLARD MOTOR CO. LTD.
STOP AUTOCRIME
S 530
SIVA 530
Designed and built by Neville Trickett Design Ltd of Blandford, Dorset
Powered by Aston-Martin 350 b.h.p., V8 engine
Epoxy resin body
Top speed: 180 m.p.h.

Right: *The Ogle Aston Martin was a fabulously opulent and advanced design, but never reached intended production as an Aston.*

Opposite page
Top: *Pictured here is the Clan as made in Northern Ireland in the mid-eighties.*

Bottom: *1971 Siva S530: adventurous prototype which was earmarked to become an Aston Martin.*

Siva

The Siva S530 could have become an Aston Martin. In the event, like so many other promising projects, absolutely nothing came of it.

Neville Trickett, creator of the Siva marque, was commissioned by the *Daily Telegraph* to produce a car for its stand at the 1971 Earl's Court Motor Show — which he duly did in just four months.

Aston Martin supplied the 5340cc fuel-injected V8 engine (which was claimed to give the car a top speed of 180mph), and Trickett the styling and construction. Features of the S530 included an unusual leather-trimmed interior with a square steering wheel and a transparent Perspex instrument nacelle, plus electric gullwing doors.

Financial difficulties prohibited Aston from putting the car into production. Trickett tried to launch the car himself with some styling revisions and a Chevrolet V8 engine, but other — and less ambitious — Siva projects took precedence.

Ogle Aston Martin

Like the Siva, the Ogle Aston Martin could also have become an exciting model made by Aston. Commissioned at the behest of a Canadian motor distributor for a show appearance, the Ogle-designed sports car was built with the support of many British firms, notably Aston Martin, who supplied the mechanical basis: a DBS platform and 5340cc V8 engine.

The car debuted at the Montreal Show in January 1972 and received a positively tumultuous reception. Its pretty glassfibre body with chrome borders featured Triplex Sundym glass — a novelty at the time — which flowed from the windscreen to the roof without a join. The interior housed two front seats with a single rear seat mounted diagonally. At the back, a 22-strong array of lights included 10 indicator lights which flashed in sequence towards the sides of the car, and 10 brake lights: the harder the braking, the more lights came on.

Aston Martin's plans to productionise the car and recoup its outlay were brought to a halt by a management reshuffle in 1972. The tobacco company, Wills, became the new sponsor and renamed the car the Sotheby Special. A second example was built by Ogle for a wealthy middle-aged lady in 1973, reputedly for nearly £30,000, but that was where the story ended. The Sotheby Special was also the last of the production Ogles.

Above: *Hollywood's brightest stars formed a queue to buy the Panther J72, which launched the marque on a voyage of increasingly odd turns.*

Panther

The name Panther conjures up all that was exciting about the specialist car business in the 1970s. It was the epitome of alternative motoring, showing just what was possible through experiment, just what the mainstream would never dare do. And, at times, it showed just how vulgar the outcome could be.

Robert Jankel was the marque's founder: a fashion designer who built one-offs. It was a one-off which began the Panther story. Inspired by a Jaguar SS100 he had seen at Beaulieu, Jankel built a replica around modern Jaguar mechanicals. A cousin also wanted one, and so did many others who saw the car.

The J72 (named after the year of its introduction, 1972) made it to the front page of *Autocar* even before its production life had begun. Beautifully handcrafted — a Panther hallmark — it was also quick, initially with the 3.8-litre XK engine and then with either a 4.2- or 5.3-litre V12. For the last of these a 0-60mph time of 4.5 seconds was recorded — at a cost of fuel consumption around 10mpg.

Panther had cracked a new market for 'retro-style' cars for sale to the very rich. The cars were not cheap (a 1973 J72 would cost from £5,285, when a Jaguar E-Type V12 could be had for £3,319), but there were customers prepared to pay for them. Within a year, 12 had been built; within two years, over 100 had found homes all over the world, their owners ranging from Arab princes to Liz Taylor. Eventually, Panther delivered a total of 422 J72s.

In 1974, as the company expanded, a new model appeared. This was the Ferrari FF, built for the Swiss firm, Felber. It would be heresy today to cut up a Ferrari 330GTC or Daytona in order to put a replica body on it, but that is exactly what Panther did. Perhaps luckily, only seven examples of the Panther FF were made, although Felber subsequently commissioned Michelotti to build a few more.

The quirkiest Panther of all was the Lazer of 1974. This extraordinary three-seater Jaguar-based beach buggy resembled a slice of finest Gruyere and was built

Right: *1974 Panther Lazer: perhaps mercifully, a one-off wedge based on a Jaguar XJ12 with the most ridiculous rear spoiler ever seen on a road car.*

Below: *Panther's attempt to create a Lancia D24 Carrera replica on a Fulvia base looked unhappy and was ill-fated.*

to special order for a Canadian customer. If nothing else, it proved that Panther would build anything as long as the customer wanted it. Ironically, in this instance the customer's wife decidedly did not want it, throwing a wobbler at her first sight of the Lazer. Panther were ordered to re-sell the car immediately.

Apart from its oversized nose, the 1975 replica of the Lancia D24 Carrera was a fine car. It was based on the Lancia Fulvia and there were plans for Lancia itself to sell a production run. However, the prototype was badly damaged in transit to the 1975 Geneva Show and Lancia failed to maintain interest in the project.

Panther's second significant model, an interpretation of the Bugatti Royale, was the enormous De Ville, first shown in 1974. Painstakingly handcrafted from aluminium, the De Ville impressively retained the excellent handling and performance characteristics of the Jaguar XJ6/12 from which its mechanical side derived. When a two-door convertible appeared in 1976, it held the questionable honour of being the UK's most expensive production car, ahead even of the Rolls-Royce Camargue at a price of £30,518. Towards the end of the De Ville's life, Panther even made a six-door version. Total production of De Villes amounted to 51 saloons and six convertibles.

The Rio was Panther's attempt, in the middle of the fuel crisis, to marry economy motoring with top-notch luxury. Based on the Triumph Dolomite or Dolomite Sprint, it is the Panther design which Robert Jankel today rates most highly. But even so, it was far too expensive to be successful, costing comfortably more than the top-of-the-range Jaguar XJ12. Production totalled just 38.

The most significant Panther model of all, because it was the firm's first attempt at a volume production car, was the Lima, shown as a prototype at the 1976 Motor Show. The Vauxhall Magnum provided the basis for this cheeky roadster, its 2.3-litre engine delivering

Above: *1976 Panther De Ville convertible was for a while Britain's most expensive production car.*

Below: *1977 Panther 6: monstrous six-wheeler was beset by problems and never ran at its claimed top speed of 200mph.*

good performance. In appearance, the Lima aped the styles of the 1930s but added some quirky features of its own such as a cheese-grater grille and hefty front spoiler. It sold well, at a rate of seven a week, boosted by the arrival in 1978 of a 178bhp turbocharged version.

Possibly the most outrageous Panther, and undoubtedly the star of the 1977 Motorfair, was the Panther 6, whose modest name merely hinted at its six-wheeled supercar format. Twin-steering front wheels utilised technology pioneered by the Tyrrell Formula One six-wheeler and supported the bulk of a twin turbocharged 8.2-litre Cadillac V8. This was quoted as delivering over 600bhp, powering the car to a claimed top speed of over 200mph. A lavish interior

***Above:** Panther Equus prototype was based on Panther's 'car for the masses', the Vauxhall-based Lima (shown in the background).*

featured three-abreast seating, LED instrument display, miniature TV and telephone.

There were numerous problems in getting the turbos to work properly, and the car's handling was dubious on hand-cut tyres. It was Pirelli's failure to supply P7 tyres which ultimately prevented a production run. Listed at £39,950, only one true Panther 6 was built, though a second was cobbled together later from parts intended for a future assembly line.

In 1978 Panther built an MG-sized sports car prototype for Vauxhall. Called the Equus, it was based on a Lima chassis but used as much hardware as possible from the Vauxhall range. Its clean lines attracted favourable comment, and *Car* magazine called it 'GM's MG basher'. When Vauxhall abandoned its plans to productionise the car, Panther bought the project but failed to get the government grant it was looking for to set up a production facility in Northern Ireland — someone else got it!

There were several other Panther projects. Of the 1977 Croisette, a one-off Ferrari Daytona-based estate, it was claimed that its turbocharged V12 engine would provide 600bhp and boot the car up to 230mph. Panther also made replica aluminium AC Cobra bodyshells, a four-door Range Rover for BL and a turbocharged Vauxhall Chevette...

In 1978, when Panther was at its zenith, it was making one De Ville, six J72s and 40 Limas each month — a total of 550 cars a year. Ultimately, though, the expansion required to manufacture the Lima extended the company to such a degree that in December 1979, when two export agents failed to make their usual payments, Panther was unable to cover its debts and went into liquidation. It was bought by Young C. Kim, a Korean tycoon, and by 1981 business had returned to normal with the De Ville, J72 and Lima all in production again. Although Jankel retained a 20 percent stake in the new firm, the paths of the two men were clearly divergent and Jankel sold his share within six months to establish the Le Marquis name. Kim's Panther assaulted the 1980s as a rather different beast, as described in Chapter Eight.

Gilbern

Carried on the success of the rather ugly 1800, Gilbern by 1970 had a modern sports saloon to compete with the big boys. The Genie of 1966 was succeeded in 1969 by the Invader, a crisper and better-handling car, though retaining its predecessor's basic lines. There was an estate version as well, which proved just as popular as the saloon: 200 of each were sold. The Invader MkIII of 1972 marked the Welsh firm's departure from kit-built cars, being the first (and last) Gilbern available only as a fully-built car. It was in fact extremely well-built and quite luxurious, and its uprated Ford three-litre V6 offered 125mph and 0-60mph in 7.2 seconds.

However, Gilbern was suffering the same problems as almost all of its kind: it was too big for lean times. The company changed hands three times in as many years, and by 1975 it had fallen into bankruptcy. A rescue bid put the Invader back in production, but when the workers staged a sit-in because of what they saw as poor management, it was obvious that the company was on its last legs. It folded finally in 1976, with around 600 Invaders of all types sold.

Probe

Few cars have ever caused such a media storm as the Probes. Dennis Adams, stylist of the Marcos 1800, decided to build the lowest car he could: his Design Probe Number 15 (shortened to Probe 15 by the press) was just 29 inches high, with passenger access via a sliding roof. An 875cc Imp engine provided the power.

When it appeared at the 1969 Racing Car Show, press agencies went berserk. The Probe 15 appeared on the front pages of newspapers from Sydney to Baghdad, and there was no shortage of rich and famous potential punters either. However, despite plans to productionise it, the Probe 15 was simply too impractical and only one was made, although a second bodyshell got a VW chassis under it later.

The Probe 16, instigated by the *Daily Telegraph* for its stand at the 1969 Motor Show, made some concessions to practicality, having an electric roof/door and five inches more height. It also had a mid-mounted BMC 1800 engine. Once again production targets were set, but only three 16s were made.

The Probe 2001 did actually make it into production. Arriving in 1970, it was now 37 inches high and sported a distinctive roof aerofoil. But after eight months and four cars, Adams' firm was on shaky ground. The last Probe (the 7000: an Oldsmobile-engined show car with a central driving position) was also dragged down when the firm collapsed.

The 2001 project was bought by a Scottish firm who had another dozen bodyshells made up to 1972.

Ironically, the most successful Probe variants were kit car derivatives called the Centaur and, later, the modified Pulsar, made from 1974 to 1982. About 50 Centaurs and Pulsars were built, all with Imp engines.

Below: *1972 Gilbern Invader MkIII: the first Gilbern sold only in complete form.*

Above: *The Adams Design Probe Number 15 was the world's lowest car, just 29 inches high.*

Right: *Dennis Adams (centre) and brother Peter (right) at the time of the ambitious Probe 15 design exercises.*

Below: *The Probe 2001 was the refined production Probe, featuring an electric sliding roof for entry.*

Above: Jaguar-based Owen Sedanca might have reached production, had not Jaguar seen it as a potential rival to its own XJ-S.

Owen Sedanca

Chris Humberstone is one of those prolific British designers who have never achieved international recognition. In a career spanning from modified Minis to his own marque, Rapport, his first entire project was the Owen Sedanca.

Commissioned by the luxury car dealer, H.R. Owen, the Sedanca was to be a sports coupé, with plenty of room for passengers. Humberstone designed an aluminium body which would fit a Jaguar XJ6 floorpan. It featured a sloping nose with pop-up headlamps, a rubber front bumper which encircled the grille, and a hatchback. The car looked good in profile, but less so from the front where there was a definite awkwardness about it.

A luxurious interior featured Dralon and suede, and even included silver hairbrushes and a silver notepad! There was more than enough space for four and, with the rear seats folded, a remarkable 34.6cu ft. of luggage space.

The car was launched in September 1973 to much acclaim and the sweet sound of 80 deposits being taken. Owen planned to make 100 cars a year; but this was exactly when the fuel crisis hit, and custom for the car swiftly evaporated. And there was another reason why the Sedanca failed to make it into production: Owen showed it to Jaguar, who returned it, refusing point blank to give it their support. The reason? A year later, the XJ-S was launched.

Both the prototype and the only production car were destroyed, and that would have been the end of it but for a rich Arab who ordered one for his son and then another for his second son, in 1978 and 1983. Both these Sedancas were completed by Robert Jankel (of Panther) and both are known to exist today.

Left: Hugely powerful GKN FFF100 was an exercise in maximum acceleration and braking potential.

GKN

Designing a car with no other purpose but to get to 100mph and back to rest as quickly as possible might seem a little frivolous. But for GKN, the automotive parts manufacturer, the GKN FFF100 was a valuable test-bed and publicity machine.

Based on a Jensen FF chassis, the 1972 FFF100 was a fireworks display of technology. Its seven-litre Chrysler engine was modified to dragster specifications to produce 620bhp. With GKN/Ferguson four-wheel drive, Maxaret anti-lock brakes and a mammoth body styled by William Towns, it was truly state-of-the-art.

When it came to the crucial 0-100-0 test, the FFF100 blasted off the line at MIRA (the Motor Industry Research Association) with minimal wheelspin, reached 100mph in just 6.5 seconds, and was back at rest in 11.5 seconds. Perhaps more remarkably, it took only 0.7 seconds longer in the wet.

Apart from appearances at Prescott Hillclimbs, that was that for the FFF100. Currently it is in the hands of a collector of Chrysler Hemi-engined cars. For GKN, the exercise was worthwhile, as a US police force subsequently ordered GKN four-wheel drive to be fitted to its Plymouth Fury patrol cars.

Lynx

The replica business was born of enthusiasts who wanted exotic cars of the past but couldn't afford them. Restoration expert Guy Black knew that only 63 Jaguar D-Types were ever built and decided, in 1974, to build his own.

His firm, Lynx Engineering, produced an aluminium body/chassis design remarkably similar to the original Jaguar and built exquisitely by Williams & Pritchard. Largely E-Type suspension was used, along with a six-cylinder E-Type engine offered in various states of tune up to 320bhp. With a 285bhp 3.8 in place, a top speed of 165mph was quoted and the Lynx was heralded as the fastest current British car.

Production began in 1975 in long-nose, short-nose and XKSS versions, at prices from £10,500 complete or £5,000 in fully-trimmed kit form. Lynx soon began to make a name for itself and by 1977 production was up to about 20 complete cars and 30 kits.

Diversification followed with a highly accurate Jaguar C-Type replica and transformations of the Jaguar XJ-S into convertible and estate forms, the latter called the Eventer. More recently, Lynx has made highly tuned versions of the XJ-S, with top speeds up to 180mph. The D-Type took something of a back seat until the company moved to new premises in St Leonard's-on-Sea, Sussex, where it relaunched the model in 1986.

Lynx launched replicas of the XKSS and lightweight Jaguar E-Type racer shortly before going into liquidation in 1992. Happily it was rescued and the full range of models was put back into production.

Below: *This fabulous recreation of the Jaguar D-Type was effected by Lynx Engineering.*

Monica

The Monica was a venture plagued with difficulties from the start.

The story began when a young French industrialist named Jean Tastevin approached Chris Lawrence (of Deep Sanderson fame) about supplying engines for a new luxury sports car. When Lawrence discovered that no designs for the car had even been formulated, he offered to design the whole thing from the ground up. This was the start of a long and tortuous partnership between Lawrence and Tastevin's firm, CFPM.

The first aluminium prototype was built in 1967, initially with a Triumph engine and then with a Martin racing V8. These were rather ugly test-beds. The Martin engines were hand-built until Coventry Victor were contracted to make a batch of 250. They went bankrupt having made only 14.

Strikes in France convinced Tastevin to search for a sub-contractor and he called upon Jensen to quote. Then Tastevin asked for a redesign by some French stylists and gave the job of making the new prototype to Vignale. This proved to be 550lbs overweight and a British firm was asked to provide an all-aluminium version.

This didn't work out either, so — back to Vignale. But Vignale was then taken over by de Tomaso, who weren't interested in the Monica. The project came almost full circle with a production line being set up in France. There were problems with engine reliability and the capacity was increased from three to 3.5 litres for extra power (240bhp).

At least production was now looking close. A French magazine opined that the Monica — named after Tastevin's wife — would be *la Jaguar Francaise*, but costings began to indicate that it would be more than twice as expensive as a Jaguar.

Finally the unreliability and lack of torque in the Martin-derived engines proved too troublesome and in 1972 the car was re-engineered to accept a 5.6-litre Chrysler V8 and was renamed the Monica 560. A 5.9-litre was also tried because the smaller engine had insufficient power, but eventually the 5.6 was used in much modified form. Even then, the car did not actually go on sale until late 1974.

The Monica was another gas-guzzler in fuel-conscious times and lasted only a few months, until February 1975. Of about 35 cars built, some 25 were prototypes.

Panther Westwinds bought the rights to the Monica with the intention of selling the car for £8,000 — roughly half what it had cost under CFPM. But it was simply the wrong car at the wrong time and no further Monicas were made.

Left: *After an enormously long development period, the Anglo-French Monica was launched with disastrous results in the middle of an oil crisis.*

Opposite page
Top: *The Mallalieu Barchetta was a fine way to turn your rusty old Bentley Mk6 into a glorious roadster.*

Below: *Mallalieu toyed with the idea of building the polar opposite of the Bentley, the tiny Microdot.*

Mallalieu

Derry Mallalieu was one of the first of the Bentley Mk6 special builders to put a special into production, and one of the most prolific. The easy availability of rusty Mk6 Bentleys and their separate chassis proved ideal for the construction of basic sports bodies and a number of firms flourished in the 1970s, building these sporting chariots for the brave few.

Mallalieu built his first special in America during the 1960s, but returned to Abingdon, Oxfordshire, with the idea of making the car in series. Using a modified Mk6 chassis, he built a fabric-covered aluminium body over an ash frame. With cycle wings, a long bonnet and right-hand gear lever, the result evoked convincing images of Bentleys in the 1930s.

The first Mallalieu, built in 1974, was a 2+2 called the Barchetta, but Mallalieu already had plans for a two-seater with flowing wings to be called the Mercia (later, the Oxford). Unfortunately, he died in 1975 and never saw the new car, which his company completed in 1976. By this time, demand for both models — especially from the USA — had made Mallalieu one of the biggest Mk6 conversion firms, if not *the* biggest.

The cars were not cheap — £9,950 for a Barchetta and £15,000 for a Mercia in 1977. But their prices reflected the time it took to hand-build the cars: four months for a Barchetta and six for a Mercia.

Without a doubt, these were impeccably conceived vehicles offering vintage grand touring without vintage reliability headaches. There were even the options of aluminium disc wheels, high-geared rear axles for touring, and a supercharger.

The company branched out in a very different direction when it announced plans to manufacture the William Towns-designed Microdot microcar. However, with its luxury specification indicating a price of £10,000, the project looked unfeasible and the idea was dropped.

In 1980 Mallalieu built a one-off for an American client, John Weitz. Called the X600, this strange-looking Camaro-based sports car looked for a time as if it might be built to special order by Mallalieu. But by early 1981 the firm was experiencing financial difficulties which led to insolvency. It left behind a legacy of several dozen delightful Bentley sports cars.

Above: *The Albany: superbly executed evocation of an Edwardian carriage.*

Albany

The Albany, which appeared in December 1971, was one of the first commercially available 'replicars' in the UK. Launched by an engineering firm from Christchurch, Dorset, with spare capacity, it elicited an immediate response from the buying public. Nothing quite like it had been seen before.

Beneath a highly convincing exterior modelled around the lines of a 1908 Buick lay nothing more archaic than Morris Minor running gear. The Minor's engine, gearbox, steering, suspension *et al.* were transplanted into a tubular chassis. A special limiter was placed on the 948cc engine just in case it should prove too raunchy for the style — top speed, 40mph.

The detail on the Albany was stunning: in true Edwardian style, everything was handcrafted, from the spoked aluminium wheels to the brass radiator surround. The price of £1,987 reflected the man hours required to build each example of the two-seater, as well as that of putting it through its 30mph crash test.

An evocative and effective brochure stated that the Albany was 'one of the most adventurous departures from conventional motor car design ever to compel the attention of gentlemen disposed towards horseless vehicular propulsion over the Queen's highway'.

In 1974, in an effort to ply export markets, the Albany was fitted with a 1493cc Triumph Spitfire engine and demeaning accessions to current legislation, such as a modern steering column. A stretched five-seater appeared in 1976, by which time over 100 two-seaters had been made. In 1979 a van arrived and proved popular for a while; but with the appearance of other, cheaper Edwardian vans, the Albany was no longer competitive. Two years later, in 1981, the company folded.

Stevens

Having been producing period-style vans around Ford Transit and Escort bases since 1972, Anthony Stevens decided to employ some spare capacity by producing a sports car. Keeping to traditional lines, in 1977 he designed and built the Sienna, a diminutive 2+2 of excellent finish and appearance.

Unable to acquire the desired Triumph Spitfire chassis from BL, Stevens instead used a lowered Reliant Kitten chassis, complete with its 848cc 40bhp engine, plus steering, brakes and front suspension. Primarily intended as a sports runabout for women, the Sienna was not a dashing performer — 80mph tops, and 0-60mph in 17 seconds. Planned to sell for £3,000, the car never went into production. It did, however, lay the ground for Stevens' next project, the Cipher.

Co-designed with Peter Bird, the prototype Cipher appeared in 1980 to widespread acclaim. Again based around Reliant Kitten mechanicals, with GRP panels hung on a separate steel frame, the Cipher even passed Type Approval tests. It was amazingly economical and could reach 90mph — some even heralded it as the Frogeye Sprite reborn. But sadly, as was so often the case, the finance needed to put the car into production did not materialise.

In 1983, as an interim measure, Stevens entrusted the Cipher to Peter Bird who would at least be able to put it on sale in kit form. At £3,500 plus taxes, the kit consisted of a rolling chassis with a brand-new engine and gearbox plus all parts needed to complete the car. Bird managed to sell a few before Stevens decided to rework the entire Cipher concept.

Responding to such comments as 'if only it had a bigger engine', Stevens redesigned the Cipher to accept a Ford power unit, enlarging the whole structure. But even this failed to excite potential financiers, and the Cipher must go down as one of the best of the many lost causes of specialist motoring.

Below: *Reliant basis for the Stevens Sienna confined it to an essentially non-sporting role.*

Above: *The attractive Stevens Cipher never made full production — a pity, as it was a thoroughly well-designed little sports car.*

Chapter Seven

The Kit Car Renaissance of the 1980s

The age of kit car experimentation had largely ended as the 1970s drew to a close. The fun had quickly gone out of beach buggies; prolific designers like Barrie Stimson and Neville Trickett were throwing in the towel; and sales of kits had declined to a very low level.

Yet from what seemed a near-unsalvageable situation, certain elements emerged which swung the industry's fortunes yet again. First, a new wave of much more professionally designed cars appeared — cars which people could actually build, instead of having to fight to get them on the road. Second, both reflecting and furthering the trend, there appeared a range of magazines devoted solely to kit cars, where formerly they had been allowed only the occasional (and with a few exceptions derogatory) mention in more conventional motoring journals. Third — and again embodying both cause and effect — regular 'kit car events' were organised which led to a further widening of enthusiasm for the breed.

The first of the new-wave quality kits was the Midas, which can be seen as the kit car *par excellence* of the '80s: small, light, with superb construction and handling, the Midas was followed by NG, UVA, Marlin, JBA and others, all offering far better standards than had been permitted in earlier years.

These models were all comprehensively recorded in a clutch of new enthusiast-led periodicals. *Alternative Cars, Kit Car, Component Car, Kit Cars & Specials, Kitcars International, Which Kit?* and others brought the kit car scene to a vast new public, as did such extravaganzas as the National Kit Car Show, the National Component Car Show, and competition events like the Kit Car Racing Series and the Historic Replica Challenge.

In 1979 there were about 40 different kits for buyers to choose from. By 1983, that had climbed to over 150. At the kit car's zenith in the middle of the decade, up to 200 different models were available at any one time, significantly greater than the choice of mass-produced cars concurrently offered.

Nor was it merely the number of models which grew: the variety, too, was incomparably greater. There were replicas, fun cars, supercars, convertibles, utility cars, off-roaders, traditional-style cars, three-wheelers — and, of course, some whacky contraptions which defied categorisation.

By far the most important of these were the replicas and traditional-style vehicles. To describe the phenomenon as a mushroom, or even an Alice in Wonderland toadstool, would be an understatement. Replicas of just about every classic and exotic car imaginable appeared during the course of the 1980s, from Ferraris and Lamborghinis to Bugattis and Jaguar E-Types. Some were controversial — Ferrari and Caterham Cars both brought court cases against copiers — some were beautifully made, and others were so inaccurate that one could hardly recognise their source.

It was indeed a decade of nostalgia. Quite apart from the painstakingly specific replicas, there were literally dozens of designs which evoked the moods and styles of the past. Usually such designs took the form of the flowing fenders and free-standing headlamps of the 1930s — at shows, it was often hard to move for running boards and mock louvres — but there were also worthy attempts to capture shades of the 1950s and 1960s.

It was also a decade of revivals. Designs which everyone thought — usually with relief — had been long dead were brought back from the grave with abandon. Mostly these were the buggies and fun cars of the 1970s for which some enterprising fellow had discovered the moulds and bravely re-entered production. Such projects were usually short-lived.

Indeed, a short lifespan continued to be the keynote of kit car firms and conspired to keep a rapidly-improving industry in disrepute. Only a handful of firms lasted more than a few years. Some lasted only a few months, if that, often leaving customers out-of-pocket with a box of unbuildable rubbish.

JBA, Marlin, GTM, DJ and others are among the most luminous of the names which have endured. Among the great casualties of the last dozen years have been UVA, Midas, Dutton and NG, their disappearance helping to reinforce the perception that there is still no such thing as a dependable kit car firm.

As the 1990s progress, the kit car industry as a whole is still thriving, with a rich variety of cars on offer. It is increasingly professional. The emergence of organisations like the Specialist Car Manufacturers Group (SCMG), part of the SMMT, has helped provide a platform for improving industry standards. Thanks to legislation coming into force in 1993, kit car manufacturers will at last be able to sell their cars fully-built, provided they pass a Low Volume Type Approval test.

Replicas continue to be the flavour of the moment, along with Lotus Seven-style roadsters and, unexpectedly, three-wheelers. As for the future, the unpredictability of the business makes forecasting a foolish business; but Eurocrats and economics permitting, the kit car movement will not die easily in Britain. The unquenchable urge to create something apart from the norm will surely keep it alive.

***Above:** Without a doubt, the Midas was the best and most credible kit car project of the 1980s, combining excellent build quality, fine dynamics and professional appearance.*

Midas

No car exemplifies the kit car revolution of the 1980s better than the Midas. It was professionally built, attractively styled by Richard Oakes, and finely engineered with handling which is near-legendary.

The project had humble origins: it was to have been an update of the Mini-Marcos produced by Harold Dermott's D&H Fibreglass Techniques. But Dermott and Richard Oakes decided to take things a stage further and build an all-new car. The Midas of 1978 was the end-result of their efforts.

Of glassfibre monocoque construction, the Midas used Mini components in a package which, quite simply, worked. It offered 2+2 accommodation, 100 percent rustproofing, superb performance/economy balance, and the sharpest handling for anything like the price.

People started queuing to buy one, including Formula One designer Gordon Murray. Soon, Midas production was up to 60 cars a year. (Most sold as rather up-market kits, the intention eventually to sell them as complete cars never being realised.) From *Motor* and *Car* magazines, the Midas won the accolade of being featured on both their front covers.

In 1986, the concept was overhauled with the new Midas Gold. A restyle by Oakes had given it a fatter stance, 'frogeye' headlamps and a bigger glass area. Gordon Murray contributed to the under-body aerodynamics; and the Metro, including the MG variants, provided the mechanical basis. Again, it was a widely acclaimed car. Meanwhile, the original Midas continued to be sold as the Midas Bronze.

The next significant development was the arrival, in 1989, of the Gold convertible. This was a fabulous-looking car — restyled by Steve Pearce — which was right in just about every respect. *Car* magazine called it the most worthwhile British sports car of the year. Cheap, fast and exhilarating, it promised to be Midas' springboard into an altogether larger league.

Yet, within a year, the firm was bankrupt. A factory fire in April 1989 only compounded its financial difficulties and in December the receivers were summoned. Only 15 convertibles had been built.

A firm called Pastiche Cars purchased manufacturing rights but built only six more convertibles before it, too, bit the dust. In 1991 well-known Midas rivals GTM bought the Midas concern. GTM relaunched the convertible and sold the Bronze to Midtec, who re-started production in 1992.

NG

Nick Green was a mechanical design student whose first car, the Tycoon, was a college project. This Rover mid-engined V8 coupé was actually offered for sale in 1979, but the prototype remained unique.

It did, however, act as a starting-point for Green's succession of traditional-style tourers, all of which were notable for their quality and engineering integrity. First of them was the TA of 1979, a rather boxy 2+2 affair with cycle wings, based loosely on the vintage Aston Martin International. With MGB bits underneath, it also had something of a vintage British sports car's character. The TA had no serious competitors at the time and sales were good.

The second NG also looked back to Aston Martin, this time to the Ulster. The 1982 TC was lower and wider than its predecessor and had only two seats, but it still relied on MGB parts, with the option of Rover V8 power. A 2+2 version, the TD, and a 2+2 with flowing wings, the TF, followed in 1983. A lightweight racing version, the TCR, arrived in 1985, followed by Rover six-cylinder (2.3 or 2.6) options for the TC, TD and TF.

This was NG's heyday: a flourishing range, healthy sales and a sound reputation, with few serious competitors. For 1985, they even mooted the possibility of producing a fully-built and very expensive enclosed Sedan. But events were catching up with them. Others were beginning to cash in on the interest in pre-war-style kits, the MGB was fast becoming a classic worth restoring, and NG lost much of its impetus.

In 1987, after over 200 had been made, the TA was sold to the TA Motor Car Co., who developed a Marina-based chassis. The rest of the range was sold in 1989 to Pastiche Cars, who picked up the TA at the same time. Each model was renamed: the TA became the International, and the TF the Ascot. This was now available with Marina parts, or, as the Gladiator, with a Rover V8. NG's final Ford Sierra/Cortina-based TF, which never really got off the ground, was marketed by Pastiche as the Henley.

Confused? So was everyone else when Pastiche went under in 1990 and the NG range was bought by GTM. The Henley passed on to Triple C, makers of the Challenger, in 1992.

Below: *The NG range in 1983: TA (left), TC (right) and TD (rear).*

Above: *William Towns (standing) was the designer of the amazing Hustler range, which included this all-wooden version.*

Hustler

Famous for his Aston Martins and for his continuous contribution to British styling, William Towns created in 1978 a novel vehicle which he called the Hustler.

It was a brilliantly simple design: a chassis/frame on to which was hung a body in two parts: the lower a series of glassfibre boxes, the upper almost entirely of glass, including the doors which slid back for entry. Beneath it all were standard Mini subframes.

Initially, Jensen Special Products were to have made the car. Then they backed out and Towns, left with a project of undeniable promise, took the bold decision to launch the Hustler as a kit car out of his own resources.

This was the beginning of a ten-year mushroom which saw the Hustler diversify into as many as 72 different variants. First there was the convertible, followed by the six-wheeled Hustler 6 and the pick-up Hobo. Amazingly, Towns also offered a plans set and glass to create an all-wooden Hustler from 1980. Next year came the cut-down Sprint and convertible Sports models, neither of which caught on.

Above: *The original Hustler prototype of 1978. Its supremely simple design included the fitment of plastic school chairs as seats!*

Below: *The most basic Hustler was the Hellcat, with an absolute minimum of bodywork and a pickup-type rear tray.*

Above: *The most extraordinary of the 72 Hustler variants was surely this eight-wheeled amphibian.*

But the Hustler idea did catch on. In 1982 came the absolute-basic Hellcat jeep (as ever, in four- or six-wheeled form) and, in 1983, the Huntsman, a restyled Hustler with Metro or Austin 1100 parts and larger-diameter wheels. 1985 brought yet another creative burst, with the Force 4 and 6, which had conventional opening doors, and the ultimate Hustler, the Highlander 6, which had Jaguar V12 power, six wheels, and was immense. Only eight were sold, however.

Towns was unstoppable. Hardly tarrying to consider whether each new derivative was commercially viable, he created the Holiday, with a Renault Espace-type front, followed by an amphibious Hustler (based on a Crayford Argocat) and a Hustler sailing-boat!

By now, though, the merry-go-round was beginning to slow. The market for Hustlers was far from infinite; by 1988 sales were falling off sharply, and within a short time the range was effectively withdrawn. Towns had not had the chance to design his Cortina-based version, with rounded edges. But a heritage of several hundred vehicles was left behind, testifying to a truly astounding period of personal creativity.

Dutton

By the end of the 1970s, Tim Dutton's stark roadsters had become the most popular kit cars available. The Phaeton (1978) was the latest incarnation and was the most sophisticated Dutton to date. Its low price was the key to its volume sales and, consequently, to Dutton's ability to diversify.

In 1980 the Sierra appeared. This was an entirely new departure, not just for Dutton but for the entire kit car industry: a chunky Richard Oakes-styled estate car design which looked as though it could go anywhere, it used Ford Escort mechanicals in a ladder frame chassis which gave the car the appearance of being 'jacked up' on stilts.

The Sierra was an instant success. Within a year sales were running at five per week, enough to fund the launch of a pick-up version in 1981 which was initially advertised in *Farmer's Weekly*! Drophead and chassis/cab versions followed shortly afterwards.

The Sierra came to wider notice with the celebrated court case instigated in 1981 by Ford, who claimed they had bagged the name for their forthcoming medium-size family car. Since Dutton was already actually using the name, though Ford had indeed registered it some years before, the court ruled a 'draw' with both firms being able to use it. But Dutton had gained valuable publicity from the case.

The Melos, launched in 1981, was again based on Escort bits and again offered a lot of car for not very much money — only £865. It was a doorless 2+2 reputed to have been designed by Richard Oakes, though in fact he appears only to have carried out some preliminary work.

With these three models Dutton was forging ahead, calling itself 'Europe's leading kit manufacturer' — no hollow claim, since from 1980 to 1984 it made no less than 4,000 kits.

In 1983 Dutton briefly took on distributorship of the Portuguese-built Moke Californian, but sales were disappointingly low. Equally unsuccessful was the 1984 Rico four-seater coupé, yet again based on the Escort. Criticisms of its ugly body and lack of refinement compared with mass-produced coupés resulted, soon after its launch, in its being made only to special order.

The Legerra of 1986 was intended as a rather up-market sports car to be sold virtually complete although, in the event, it was sold as a basic kit too. It had doors, rather unusually for a Dutton, but its styling left much to be desired.

By now there were cracks appearing in the Dutton empire. The market was moving towards more sophisticated cars while, at the same time, there were many more budget cars to compete with the range. Duttons also had a reputation for questionable quality. Sales of the long-in-the-tooth Phaeton were falling away, the once top-selling Sierra was being overtaken by the Rickman Ranger, and sales of the Melos were never more than mediocre.

Dutton fought back by reviving the ancient B-Plus and launching the 1986 Rico Shuttle — a sort of Rico/Sierra hybrid laughingly dubbed a 'space van' — and the Beneto/Hacker estate kit. But the name had lost its magic: in 1989, faced with spectacularly declining sales and declaring himself 'utterly pissed off with the kit car business', Tim Dutton wound the company up. The rights to kit manufacture were sold to a number of other firms — the Phaeton to Eagle, the Melos and Legerra to Mantis Cars (later to Scorhill), and the Beneto and Sierra to Hamilton.

Dutton himself went on to launch the Hacker Maroc (1991), a fully-built open four-seater based on the Ford Fiesta Mk2. His legacy was two decades and thousands of examples of cheap and mostly cheerful alternative transport, and memories of what was at one stage the largest enterprise of its kind.

Right: *Dutton's Sierra was an inspired model: the first-ever true kit-form estate, it looked 'right' and sold in huge quantities.*

Below: *1984 Dutton Rico: an attempt at a four-seater coupé which was too unrefined to succeed.*

Left: *The Eagle SS owed its parentage to the Nova but was rather more practical with its gullwing doors.*

Eagle

'The Eagle has landed' proclaimed the adverts in 1981, as Britain's newest gullwing exotic kit was launched. The event, in fact, was the arrival in Britain of the American Cimbria SS, a car which resembled the home-grown Nova... and the force behind the Eagle SS, as the UK-made version was known, was Alan Breeze, a cousin of the aforementioned Tim Dutton.

A VW Beetle chassis was the almost inevitable underpinning for the Eagle, whose low-slung appearance and gullwing doors won it all the friends it needed. Within a year, 100 kits had been sold, including exports. This gave Eagle the capacity to launch a 2+2 open version in 1983 and to take over another kit project, the Rhino, which was a Beetle-based open jeep. Eagle christened it the RV and within months had developed a Cortina-based chassis both for it and for the SS.

Flushed by its sales successes (300 kits a year by the mid-1980s), in 1985 Eagle developed a Land Rover-based RV to give it true 4x4 off-road ability. Then it embarked on the ambitious Milan 2+, in collaboration with a Germany company. Based on Sierra parts, this 1987 project was intended as a sophisticated 2+2 open sports car, but came to nothing. Equally unproductive was Eagle's assumption of the Welsh Hensen M30 and M70 projects, rather ugly Granada-based coupés.

Eagle's status as one of the most popular — if not the best-quality — kit firms was enhanced when it took on the Dutton Phaeton after the dissolution of the Dutton concern in 1989. Renamed the P21 (rounded front arches) and P25 (swept front arches), the models received minor improvements. Eagle's current range consists of the SS, RV and P21/25.

Merlin

The Merlin was another kit of American origin, although the UK manufacturer, Thoroughbred Cars, modified its design and offered a separate chassis for Cortina parts as well as the VW Beetle-based version when it arrived in 1980.

Very pretty — some would say the prettiest of all the neo-classic styles — it was low, wide and seductively rakish. It struck a chord with British buyers and soon had a devoted following.

The oddly named Merlin Monro of 1983 was the 2+2 version, but its appearance didn't prevent the company from folding the following year. The model was revived, however, when the old management formed Paris Cars. The Monro was mercifully named the +2, and the Merlin remains available today.

Marlin

Paul Moorhouse was a special builder *extraordinaire* and his Marlin was the vehicle which, in 1979, persuaded him to go into manufacture. Unusually, it combined aluminium and glassfibre body panels over a tubular chassis initially designed to accept Triumph Herald/Vitesse parts. The Marlin's excellence of engineering and its neat, compact design gained swift approval.

By 1981, Marlin Engineering had launched a kit based on Marina parts which offered doors as an option and became the definitive version. Alfa Romeo engines were also commonly squeezed under the bonnet. Within two years, a remarkable total of almost 150 kits had been produced. A year later, production was up to four cars a week.

1984 brought the launch of the family Marlin, called the Berlinetta. Much larger, with four seats and sporting a new body style, the Berlinetta used the Cortina as its basis, with Sierra and Fiat engines following.

That the Marlin range has enjoyed continuing success to the present day speaks volumes for the quality of the cars. So does the remarkable statistic that approximately half of all Marlin owners feel sufficiently enthusiastic about their cars to have joined the owners club.

Right: *1980 Merlin: a very handsome two-seater which was designed in America but enjoyed considerable success in Britain.*

Right: *The oddly named Merlin Monro offered 2+2 accommodation in an attractive body.*

Below: *Excellent engineering and an unusually pretty body distinguished the Cornish Marlin.*

***Above:** Alongside its enduringly popular range of buggies GP also launched the Talon sports coupé.*

GP

Britain's biggest buggy company, GP, was ready to assault the new decade with one invaluable ingredient: the extraordinary talents of designer Neville Trickett.

Trickett had exhausted the possibilities of his Siva marque by the end of the 1970s, but still had one new idea to try out. His scheme was to create a Packard-influenced roadster in miniature for a VW chassis — enough to make most enthusiasts cringe. But the resulting Madison was an undoubted triumph.

A curious mixture of flowing curves and traditional touches, the Madison had an ostentatious sense of humour. Trickett planned to sell the car through his own company, Ground Effect Developments (a name which reflected his interest in hovercraft), in 1980.

By 1981, however, the project had effectively been taken on by GP, with Trickett a director. Trickett's GP connection had begun with the Kubel and then the 1979 Talon, an attractive 2+2 gullwing coupé which GP had asked him to design. The Talon was not a great success, only 30 being made before a big Mk2 revamp in 1983 gave it more rear space.

It was the Madison which established itself as GP's best-seller, attracting several celebrity buyers. Supplemented by the pretty but claustrophobic Madison Coupé and a Ford Cortina-based chassis in

***Below:** The Neville-Trickett-designed GP Madison was a Beetle-based pastiche of pre-war styles whose humour shone through.*

***Above:** Launched in 1982, the very well-made JBA Falcon was based on Ford Cortina parts.*

1983, the model enjoyed increasing popularity.

By that time, though, GP had another model to challenge it: the Spyder. This was a Trickett-developed replica of the classic Porsche 718 RSK racer based (suitably for once) on a shortened VW chassis. It was a beautiful re-creation, its low screen, head fairing and utter impracticality a winning combination. By the end of 1984, demand for the Spyder was outstripping that for the earlier Madison, both having reached a total of 250.

Throughout the 1980s GP also plugged away with its beach buggies; indeed, it was virtually the sole purveyor of these relics of the 'fun boom' days. They sold to resorts and to Arab customers and even enjoyed something of a national revival as, perhaps, the ozone layer rolled back to let in more sun. The Kubel, meanwhile, had died quietly during the decade's earlier years.

GP sold the Ford-based Madison to the Madison Sportscar Company, keeping the VW version itself and thereafter concentrating almost solely on VW-based kits: Spyder, Madison and buggies. The only other GP project of the 1980s was the Camel, a VW-based jeep intended for sale to third world countries, though none ever bought it.

JBA Falcon

JBA Engineering effectively launched its Falcon on ITV's *News at Ten* at the end of 1982 and after a long development period. A Cortina-based traditional roadster, it instantly won praise as a well-engineered and good-looking kit having the distinction of aluminium and GRP body panels. (It was even described as 'a Panther J72 for the working man'.) Later, Rover V8 power became an option and sales rose to five cars a month. A hardtop followed in 1984.

In 1985 JBA's second model, the Javelin, appeared. This was a Capri-based open four-seater which actually shared identical bodywork with the Capri from the waist down, albeit in GRP. It offered full four-seat open motoring and instantly won orders. But it was a labour-intensive car to make and was dropped after just a few years.

The Falcon range continued to grow, with the appearance first of a +2 version (later the Tourer) and then in 1989 a lower, wider and prettier two-seater called the Sports. The development of all-GRP bodies made production more cost-effective and the Falcons today continue to merit both respect and popularity.

Dax

DJ Sportscars has come a long way since it developed a basic glassfibre AC Cobra replica bodyshell in two halves for a German customer, back in 1979. The Dax, as the marque became known, sired most of the other 427 Cobra replicas in Europe and was by far the most successful of the numerous firms offering such replicas.

Things started slowly, with basic shells which customers were supposed to fit to their own chassis. But it wasn't long before DJ developed a choice of chassis for either Ford or Jaguar axles and 'any engine' up to American V8s. Being the first 427 Cobra manufacturer, DJ carried out most of the donkey-work of developing the idea but reaped the rewards in strong sales.

Along with every other Cobra progenitor, DJ was forbidden by Ford to use the Cobra name. Luckily, though, the company had made contact with John Tojeiro, who had been heavily involved with the original AC Ace/Cobra. He became the technical director of DJ, endorsing the car so that it became known as the Dax Tojeiro.

Developments embraced the option of ladder or 'supertube' spaceframe chassis and the fitment of a Jaguar V12 engine for stonking performance. A 289 version, with its arches cut back like those of the early original Cobra, was also offered, though with little success.

With over 1,100 sold to date, the Dax has now outstripped the sales of the car it duplicates: the AC Cobra sold just 1,070 units.

DJ diversified massively throughout the 1980s, dabbling with the Charger project of the previous decade, the Mongoose hot rod, the Nevada off-road rail and the Californian Speedster, a sort of 'blancmange mould' version of the classic Porsche Speedster, which sold in tiny numbers.

The Dax 40, a KVA GT40 replica bodyshell fitted to DJ's spaceframe chassis, appeared in 1989. The usual V8 engine/Renault transaxle configuration was used.

In 1991 DJ entered into a collaboration with Mohr Automobile of Germany and began manufacture of the German firm's Rush, a Lotus Seven-type roadster based on the Ford Cortina. For drivers who dared, even a Sierra Cosworth engine and gearbox could be fitted.

To cap it all, in 1992 DJ began offering the Covin coupé and cabriolet, two Porsche 911 lookalikes, together with the Covin Speedster acquired from the original manufacturer.

Below: *DJ Sportscars' Dax Cobra (later the Tojeiro) became the UK's definitive AC Cobra replica. Sales have overtaken those of the original.*

Moss

Moss was a company which achieved its success by being the first of the many. Its initial models unashamedly attempted to provide the charms of the Morgan at a fraction of its price.

John Cowperthwaite was a prolific special builder whose one-off based on a Triumph Herald created so much interest that in 1981 he launched it in kit form. Using a slightly modified Herald or Vitesse chassis, the Moss was easy to build, fairly cheap, and undeniably good-looking.

1983 brought two new models. The first was the Malvern, basically a 2+2 version of the original car, which became known as the Roadster. The second was the all-new Mamba, a vaguely 1960s-style open sports car of rather odd lines, again based on a Herald/Vitesse chassis. Later that year a chassis for Ford engines became available for all models.

In 1984 came the remarkable Monaco, a sort of cigar with cycle wings which could be described as a barrel of laughs at a very cheap price, but proved highly popular. Herald underpinnings or Moss' Ford-based chassis could be used.

As had happened to other companies, Moss began to lose its momentum as competitors arrived in a field it had previously had almost to itself. A factory fire in 1985 destroyed the Moss moulds and effectively brought the Cowperthwaite years to an end. He went on to create the JC marque of plans-built cars, which also briefly revived the Malvern, Roadster and Monaco in 1986, before being sold on to Hampshire Classics. Eventually, the Moss rolling stone came to rest in the caring hands of three Moss Owners Club members in Bath, where production of the Moss range continues.

Top: *Although not outstanding in any way, the Moss was a best-seller by virtue of being the first kit car to cash in on the popularity of the Morgan.*

Above: *Whether perceived as hilarious or hideous, the Moss Monaco provided many would-be pilots with flies-in-the-teeth motoring for next to no outlay.*

Above: *UVA's Fugitive range offered the bare basics in an often startlingly quick formula. This F30 could reach 60mph from rest in under five seconds.*

UVA

Alan Arnold's Unique Vehicle & Accessory Co. (UVA) was formed in late 1981 to import VW performance parts from the United States. It was on one of his visits there that Arnold acquired the UK rights to the Manta Montage, a McLaren M6 replica based on, ahem, a VW Beetle chassis.

The Montage was a stunningly styled creation which sold for a very elevated price in Britain, so sales of only seven VW-based kits in total were no worse than expected. The arrival in 1986 of UVA's own chassis into which a Rover or other V8 could be fitted gave sales the fillip they needed. With some body redesign, the new model was called the M6 GTR. UVA also hoped to make the South African-designed Badsey Bullet three-wheeled supercar, but this plan failed to materialise.

UVA's main business was Beetles, of course; it offered a Baja Bug bodykit and an estate conversion called the Shogan, both of which originated in America. A logical progression, again based on an American idea, was the Fugitive series, born in 1984. The first Fugitive was a typical off-road rail which was honed for road use and used a Beetle engine. Its main attraction was its low price — UVA claimed that a complete car could be built for under £1,000 — and it was plainly aimed at the Dutton buyer. It sold 100 examples within six months.

The (unwise) fitment of Rover V8s by customers into their Fugitives led UVA to design a proper mid-engined version specifically for V8s. The resultant F30 (1985) was a minimalist's dream with quite stunning performance: UVA claimed that it would exceed 150mph. The following year the F33 Can-Am arrived with more enclosed, but rather ugly, bodywork in the same mid-engined chassis. At the same time, a four-seater Fugitive 4 based on the old VW-based design was intended to cater to families!for

This was the range which carried UVA through to the next decade. With its strong reputation for quality and active participation in the improvement of the industry through the SCMG, the firm enjoyed several healthy years. But in 1991 it was overtaken by financial troubles and its range was transferred to a new firm, TAG, which offered UVA's into 1992.

Opposite page
The Tora was made by Ginetta, but was so different from its sports car norm that it was marketed under the name GRS.

Ginetta

Ginetta is a concern unique in this book, having a firm place in almost every chapter. In the 1980s it turned back to its roots by once again offering kit-form cars, but trained those roots in a new direction with a range of generally larger and more practical vehicles.

As 1980 dawned, Ginetta was still soldiering on with its old range. It re-introduced the G15 (last made in series in 1974) in fully-trimmed kit form, but takers were few. There were two developments of the G21, 170 of which had been made between 1971 and 1978: the G23 was a convertible version and the G24 a smoothed-out coupé, but neither reached intended production.

Then, in 1981, Ginetta relaunched an old favourite, the G4. Dubbed the G4 Series IV, it looked even lovelier than the original and had Ford Kent engines and a roomier cockpit. It took Ginetta into an area where, since the demise of MG, there was precious little competition.

Ginetta's next project, in 1982, was such a departure from its norm that it was known by a different name: GRS. The GRS Tora was a utility estate in the Matra Rancho idiom based on Hillman Hunter parts, including its doors and interior. Its spaciousness and ease of build made it by far the best kit of its type and helped it to a production rate of six per week within six months. (Its popularity subsequently waned and, shortly after launching a restyled Cortina-based Tora with four doors, Ginetta sold the rights to the project in 1989.)

Unusually, Ginetta's next sports car, which was launched at the 1983 Motorfair, was a mid-engined two-seater. The G25 was a Fiesta-based coupé which, although offered for sale, never entered production. But it did inspire the later G32.

The continuing quest for practical transport led in 1984 to the G26. A full four-seater, it was attractively styled, beautifully engineered as always, and easy to build using Cortina parts. Such was its popularity that production levels at Ginetta's Witham factory reached an all-time high. In time, the G26 spawned a notchback 2+2 version, with fixed headlamps, called the G28. Also available were the new front on the G26 (called the G30) and the pop-up headlamp front on the 2+2 (called the G31).

In the meantime, the G4 had been pepped up in 1985 and renamed the G27, with revised suspension, a big choice of engines up to Rover V8, and new frontal treatment with pop-up headlamps. It also effected Ginetta's re-entry into works racing after an absence of many years.

Ginetta's most important newcomer for many years was the G32. Despite being shown at the 1986 Birmingham Motor Show, it took three years before the car was released to the buying public. Thanks to the success of its kit-form cars — the greatest Ginetta had ever enjoyed — it could again afford to tackle the fully-built market. The Walklett brothers sold the company in 1989, just as the G32 was making its mark, and the story is continued in this book's next chapter.

Westfield

The rise of Chris Smith's Westfield sports cars from humble origins to the most successful range of the '80s is one of the decade's most remarkable stories.

The Westfield marque began with the launch of its Lotus Eleven replica in 1983. Using Midget mechanicals, it was an accurate and beautifully-made replica — though, at £3,235, expensive in kit form. British customers showed little interest, but buyers in America and Japan helped fund the next Westfield, a replica of the Lotus Seven, later the same year. Again it was based on Spridget bits, though Ford or Mazda rotary engines could also be fitted.

The Westfield Seven was a great success, hugely undercutting the price of the Caterham Seven. That, and its unrestrained duplication of the Lotus Seven, led Caterham Cars, the holders of the rights to Lotus Seven production, to take Westfield to court. Caterham won, after a long battle, in 1987, forcing Westfield to redesign and rename its car. The early models became known as 'pre-litigation cars'.

The happy outcome of this enforced return to the drawing-board was the Westfield SE. Now all-GRP, with more rounded lines, it continued where the Seven had left off, selling in fantastic numbers. An independent rear-end model, the SEi, boosted trade further; so did the 1991 SEiGHT, a Rover V8-powered version, which was claimed to reach 60mph from rest in four seconds! The 'Weasel' (1992), a Ford turbo diesel-engined SE, was probably the first diesel sports car sold as a road car, though to date no-one has bought one..

Other Westfield projects were the bizarrely-styled and unsuccessful Sports 2000, principally a competition car; the stillborn Topaz coupé of 1988; and the revised Eleven, known simply as the Sports, of 1990. This had a spaceframe chassis for Ford components.

It is the SE models which have kept the Westfield torch burning into the 1990s. To date, over 4,500 of these spartan roadsters have been sold, with no indication that demand for them will fall. Westfield launched its first fully-built model, the ZEi, at the 1992 Birmingham Motor Show, with production to start in 1993 — adding a new dimension to the decade's greatest story.

Above: *Teal's front-engined Bugatti Type 35 replica became increasingly convincing and up-market.*

Opposite page
The Westfield SE was perhaps the most winning formula of the 1980s, attempting to offer Lotus Seven-style motoring for a fraction of the cost — and succeeding.

Teal

Bugatti Type 35 replicas are to be found all over the world, but the Teal was special for two reasons: it was front-engined, where almost all others suffered with VW Beetle chassis and engines; and it was engineered with great expertise.

The classic Type 35 Bugatti is a fabulous-looking car and Ian Foster's Trafford Engineering Automotive Ltd (TEAL) produced a superb copy. Based on Morris Marina parts, largely because the antiquated suspension looked right, the original Teal used a GRP body. Later models became steadily more refined, sporting beautifully hand-made aluminium bodies and period 18-inch wheels.

A four-seater version (not a Bugatti original!) was introduced in 1986, and two years later there followed a special-order-only Type 44 replica. In 1991 the first of a limited edition of Bugatti Type 59 replicas appeared. Based on Jaguar mechanicals and hand-built to an exceptionally high standard, these up-market machines were initially sold under the GPB name.

BRA

Beribo Replica Automobiles (BRA) was probably responsible for the first British-built AC Cobra replica. John Berry and Peter Ibbotson began working on the project in 1977 and had it ready for public consumption by 1981.

The big difference was that it was a 289 replica with restrained wheel arches, at a time when almost everyone else was churning out 427s. The prototype was rather bare, with simple aeroscreens, and had a somewhat out-of-place chin spoiler which was soon abandoned. Based around MGB components, it wasn't long before a Rover V8-powered version became available. A reputation for quality workmanship provided BRA with a healthy customer base.

In 1984 BRA launched the J-Type, a two-seat roadster inspired by the 1930s MG Midget, with a chassis designed to accept MGB or Ford engines. Again it was of excellent quality, if a little pricey. The P-Type, which appeared the following year, was basically a J-Type with flowing wings.

Also launched in 1984 was BRA's 427 Cobra replica. This was created by Gerry Hawkridge (later of Transformer Cars and Hawk), using his own platform chassis, Jaguar suspension and Rover V8 engine, though Ford and American V8s could also be installed. It was sold to a German firm in 1987.

Sales continued at a regular but slow pace until, in 1992, BRA put up for sale the rights to its J- and P-Types, leaving the 289 as its sole model. Then BRA launched a new trike with Honda motorcycle engines in the Triking/JZR mould; the model was known as the CX3 Super Sports.

Left: *BRA offered the first replica of the narrow wheel arch AC Cobra 289 in 1981.*

Below: *Designed to accept MGB or Ford engines, BRA's J-Type was inspired by the 1930s MG Midget.*

Right: *The car which out-Duttoned Dutton: the Pilgrim Bulldog was basic, but offered good quality at an amazingly low price.*

Below: *Pilgrim's Sumo was the first successful attempt to market a budget Cobra replica. It used the humble Cortina as its basis. This example used a Ford Scorpio engine.*

Pilgrim

Pilgrim GRP began in the most unpromising fashion. A picture of the prototype was pushed through the letterbox of a kit car magazine the author was working for in 1984. It resembled a very large pram.

Luckily, Den Tanner, the car's designer, met up with sculptor and glassfibre wizard Bill Harling, who had been responsible for much of the decor at Heathrow and some of the stage sets for rock supergroup Yes. Harling redesigned the car and the resulting Bulldog, although hardly pretty, was at least presentable enough for the relaunch.

Morris Marina mechanicals and no doors may not sound an exciting recipe, but the Bulldog caught on instantly. The reason? Nowhere else could you buy a body/chassis kit with anything like the Pilgrim's quality for just £876. More than 40 were sold in under six months and the figures continued to rise after doors became available and the rather odd front and rear were restyled.

The next model, in 1986, was a 50s/60s-style open two-seater which went through more changes of name than a Monster Racing Loony Party candidate. Called the Swift, then the Rapier and, finally, the Hawthorn, it too was based on the Marina. But it failed to match the sales of the Bulldog and was relegated to special-order-only status.

Pilgrim then joined the Cobra fray with the Sumo, based on Ford Cortina bits. The basic concept was gradually refined, with chassis developments and V6 or V8 power options, and soon it took over from the Bulldog as the firm's mainstay. Also on offer was the MX2, a Lancia Stratos replica which used a mid-mounted Ford Escort CVH engine.

Meanwhile the Bulldog continued to develop. A Cortina chassis widened its appeal, as did the four-seater Family Tourer, new in 1989. Due to its continued low price, the Family Tourer is still one of the industry's big sellers.

Noble

Lee Noble built his Ultima with the intention of bringing race car design on to the street, forming Kitdeal Ltd to sell the design.

The Group C-inspired sports car arrived in 1985 to widespread acclaim, its fabulous chassis proving capable of extraordinary cornering powers. The first cars used Renault 20/30 power train combinations, and an Ultima took the Kit Car Racing Series twice.

Not content to rest on his laurels, in 1987 Noble launched the more curvaceous Ultima Mk3, with engine options up to large centrally-mounted V8s. But this car always took second place to other projects and in 1990, when the firm's name was changed to Noble Motorsport, it was withdrawn from sale.

Principal among these other projects was the Mk4, a replica of the 1967 Ferrari P4 endurance racer. Accurate down to the last captivating curve, the GRP-and-Kevlar kit could be built for around one-hundredth of the cost of one of the three original P4s, which have changed hands for more than £1 million. Fine quality, a lovely chassis and exhilarating performance from the Renault V6 or Rover V8 kept Noble's order book full.

The Noble 23 was another copy, this time of the Lotus 23. Using a spaceframe chassis and four-cylinder Ford power, it distinguished itself on the track as well as being offered for road use.

In 1992 the P4 passed on to JH Classics, where it became known as the Deon MkIV.

Beauford

The Beauford was another great success story of the 1980s. When first seen in 1985, it aroused some wry comments through its use of a Mini bodyshell mated with metal panels to bring about a 'neo-classic' four-seater with an impressively long bonnet and flowing wings. It used Cortina mechanicals in a ladder chassis.

The effect was imposing and the Beauford immediately found its niche, frequently as a wedding car. Within two years of its launch, it was redesigned as a GRP tub in open form, with soft and hard tops: it now looked better, and sold better. With engine options expanding to encompass the Rover V8 and Nissan straight six, and a continuing emphasis on quality, the Beauford enjoyed continuing success. New in 1992 was a four-door tourer version.

Opposite page
Ferrari made just three examples of the racing P4; over 100 enthusiasts have bought Noble's glorious copy of the car.

Right: *Wedding hire companies and lovers of the Roaring Twenties lapped up the Beauford. Note the Mini doors and windscreen.*

Below: *The addition of a four-door touring version of the popular Beauford significantly extended its appeal.*

LOMAX
Q508 FAD

Lomax

Despite being pooh-poohed by commentators who had never driven a 2CV in their lives, the idea of a 2CV-based kit was inspired. Nigel Whall was the instigator behind the ingenious Lomax range, based almost entirely on the Citroen 'A' series floorpans.

The first of the Lomax range appeared in 1983, with cyclecar-type styling inspired by the Morgan Super Sports. It used an unmodified 2CV/Dyane/Ami floor-pan with the 602cc engine. Although developing only 31bhp, in a car weighing only 8cwt, this was enough to make the car a fairly zippy performer.

This first Lomax was known as the 224, signifying two cylinders, two seats and four wheels. It followed that the 223 which came hot on its heels had just three wheels, a transformation achieved by the simple expedient of removing the Citroen rear swinging arms and turning one of them the other way round. The 223 looked cheeky and was the model which most customers chose — including the author.

There was also a fearsome 424 which used the four-cylinder Ami Super as its base; 55bhp gave it startling performance. A four-seater option was offered on all models, including the 223.

Lomax branched out with the Deja Vu, a jeep-style vehicle again based on the 2CV range, which offered a wide variety of body styles but was not as popular as the retro-sportsters.

In 1992, Lomax announced the Supa Vee. This extraordinary three-wheeler used aluminium and GRP body panels in 223 body style but mounted on a lightweight chassis of Lomax's own design. Its most interesting feature was its engine: one quarter of a Chevrolet V8, the V-twin layout provided up to 140bhp for lightning performance. Also in 1992, Lomax took over the manufacture of the Rickman range of utility estates. This, said Lomax, made them the UK's largest kit car manufacturer.

Opposite page
The Morganesque Lomax 223 three-wheeler sat atop a Citroen 2CV chassis and proved by far the most popular of the Lomax range.

This page
Above: *With its Chevrolet Vee-Twin engine fitted in a special chassis, the Supa Vee was the ultimate Lomax.*

Right: *The Lomax 224 (prototype pictured here) used the same bodyshell as the 223 but used an unmodified Citroen 2CV chassis with four wheels.*

SOB 631S

Triple C

The Triple C (Car Care Clinic) Challenger came into being when the company's founder, Derek Robinson, tried to build a Countess E-Type replica and found it a thoroughly miserable contraption. Deciding he could do better (he could hardly do worse), he created his own interpretation of the E-Type in roadster form in 1985.

To keep costs down, it was based around Cortina parts, which meant that the styling was not 100 percent convincing. As the project progressed, however, it became much closer to E-Type spec; the introduction of a Jaguar-based chassis in 1986 was the biggest single advance in the creation of a highly accurate replica. Quality was never less than excellent and sales were good.

In 1991 Triple C launched an off-road/leisure car called the Malibu — soon renamed the Tiger — and a Cunningham lightweight E-Type replica. In 1992, they took over the rights to the Henley (previously the NG TF). But financial troubles overcame the original manufacturers and in 1992 production rights were transferred to a new company, Challenger Automotive Developments, in Scotland.

Opposite page
The Triple C Challenger was a close replica of the Jaguar E-Type, eventually available with Jaguar power.

Foers

Unlike most kit cars, which are today launched in a relative blaze of publicity, the Foers Nomad was in existence for four years before being 'discovered' by the press in 1981. By then, through word of mouth alone, 28 had been sold.

This gives some idea of the attractions of this little Moke-style car, based on Mini subframes. Unusually for a kit car, the bodywork was all-metal. Three models were offered: a convertible, a pick-up and a van. By 1984, sales had risen to 120.

In 1985 came the Triton, a sleeker-looking four-seater utility car based on Metro mechanicals, again with steel-and-aluminium bodywork. Rather more civilised, but no less tough, it never matched the Nomad's sales.

Foers' last project was the Ibex, an alloy-bodied off-roader based on the Land-Rover. In 1990, John Foers sold the rights to the Nomad and Triton to Del Tech Ltd., so that he could concentrate on the Ibex alone.

Below: *Its utilitarian charm made the Foers Nomad a popular choice, even during the four years which passed before the press recognised it.*

Eurocco

Although the Eurocco never sold in any great numbers, it was perhaps available in a greater variety of forms than any other kit car. Its origins lay with Mike Carlton's Embeesea Cars, makers of the Charger, in 1978. The initial two-seater design was by Richard Oakes, but tinkering was already underway and the first Eurocco appeared in 1979 as a 2+2 notchback coupé using a standard Beetle chassis.

Demand for the Charger held back the Eurocco until 1981, when the first shells were sold in modified fastback guise. Unfortunately the door glass could not be obtained, so — back to the drawing-board. A new Eurocco was designed, with glass in the previously blank rear three-quarter panel, and went on sale in 1982. Meanwhile, the original notchback moulds had been sold to a firm called Steaney who introduced the model later in the year as the SN1. Its tiny rear seats were taken from a lawn-mower! In turn, it passed on to Amplas Ltd.

In 1984 the SN1 passed to Pulsar Cars (also known as Lemazone) who renamed it the Comet. Lemazone's restyle was never productionised before the Comet returned to the void from whence it had come in 1987.

Back to the Eurocco and yet more intrigue. Roy Coates was one of those who had bought an original Eurocco with the fastback but no rear three-quarter window. Coates built his car up to a very high standard and eventually set up a firm called S&R Sports Cars to go into production in 1985, buying up the old moulds and rights from the now-renamed MBC Cars, who had given up on the Eurocco 2. Coates introduced the SR1 two-seater and SR2 2+2, but (you guessed it) almost as soon as they were introduced, they bowed out. End, absolutely, of the Eurocco story.

Above: *Debuting in 1979, the Eurocco had probably the most tortuous history of any kit car. This is a 1982 version.*

Opposite page
Top: *The tiny Impala owed its size to the Fiat 500/126 on which it was based. Despite being both cheap and practical, it did not last long.*

Middle: *The Birchfield Sports of 1985 offered a stunning return to the days of hand-formed wings and louvres.*

Impala

The cute and cuddly Impala was the first UK kit to be based on the Fiat 500/126, arriving at the end of 1981 from Foulkes Developments. With Moke-like styling and very diminutive dimensions, it enjoyed a brief popularity. It was cheap, at £627 all in, and it was practical, too, with four seats and full weather equipment. A restyled version with round wheel arches which appeared in 1984 was not enough to sustain interest in the model; it vanished soon afterwards, taking a prototype 126-based 2+2 coupé with it.

Birchfield

Many people regarded the Birchfield Sports as the best kit car ever, when it arrived in 1985. Based on a 1982 one-off by Nick Topping, it was brought to production by ex-Panther man Clive Smart, of CV Shapecraft.

The supremely elegant lines of the Birchfield were clearly inspired by the Jaguar SS100, although it was not a replica. Based on a spaceframe chassis with a massive central spine, it used Jaguar XJ6 mechanicals which gave it superb road manners.

Its most magnificent feature was its handcrafted aluminium body. Each rear wing consisted of three separate sections which needed no filling before painting; the chromed brass radiator had nine pieces; and the bonnet had 280 individually-pressed louvres.

A typical price of £12,000 for a completed car made the Birchfield the most *expensive* kit car of the time. For a fortunate few it made a fabulous project, but it proved too uneconomic to produce and was withdrawn from sale in 1987, along with the firm's Lotus racer replica, the SR, which became the Noble 23.

Falcon

Lotus Seven-style vehicles were a constant theme of the 1980s, but surely the unlikeliest member of the group was the 2CV-based Falcon S. Peter Bird was its creator, a man whose background included the marketing of both the Stevens Cipher and the Lomax.

The Falcon S was the second Bird project (a pair of abortive multi-purpose vehicles called the Quarry and the Chase had preceded it) and was launched in 1984. Using the 2CV/Dyane floorpan, its styling was convincing, but its performance was never on a par with its looks. The body was of plywood-and-aluminium sandwich with GRP wings and offered 2+2 accommodation. The basic kit cost just £406, and if that was too expensive then Falcon Design would sell you a set of plans for £10 so that you could built your own vehicle from scratch.

A boat-tail three-wheeler version arrived in 1986 along the same lines as the Falcon's principal rival, the Lomax. Eventually, Peter Bird passed on the project to a new firm in Stratford.

Sherwood

The Spartan Car Company successfully weathered the whole of the 1970s and 1980s with its popular MG TF-style kit. With the Sherwood (1984), it branched out in a totally new direction, forming a separate company to make and market it.

The Sherwood was a large estate car/pick-up which cleverly used the centre section of a Ford Cortina in its own chassis, on to which 14 separate GRP panels bolted. This didn't make for an easy build-up, but the kit was economically priced and sold in reasonable numbers. A five-door version was also offered.

The Sherwood was followed by the monstrous Starcraft, a six-wheeled motor caravan in kit form, with Cortina or P100 pick-up basis. Again, its low price created acceptable sales.

Above: *You would never guess that a Citroen 2CV lay beneath the Lotus Seven-style Falcon S.*

Below: *Launched in 1984, the Sherwood emerged from the Spartan stable.*

***Above:** Rickman's Ranger stole all of Dutton's thunder with its much better quality multi-purpose kits.*

Rickman

The name Rickman will be familiar to motorcycle enthusiasts as that of a successful British 'bike manufacturer. Experience in glassfibre, and in making chassis and bodies for both Eagle and Brightwheel, led Rickman in 1987 to create the Ranger kit car. With the Dutton Sierra as its only (and rather less refined) competitor, the Rickman Ranger was well placed to take the largest slice of the kit utility cake, which it duly did.

Based, like the Dutton, on Escort mechanicals, the Rickman came in estate and soft-top forms and was a far more convincing rival than Dutton for the Suzuki SJ and other mass produced jeep-style vehicles. In particular, its all-GRP bodywork was first-class.

Variants followed soon after: the Rancher was a mini motorhome and the Space Ranger a longer and wider Ranger into which Ford engines of up to two litres could be fitted. Rangers sold in their hundreds and became the industry benchmark for this type of vehicle.

Rickman's Métisse of 1990 was an altogether different project. A 2+2 sports coupé, it was based on the Ford Sierra, from which it also took its two doors and much of its interior. The finesse of its engineering can be gauged from the fact that Ford offered technical assistance with the project. Very much up-market, priced at £7,030 in kit form, the emphasis was on complete cars. In 1992, a steam-powered Métisse was being prepared to assault the land speed record for steam-driven vehicles.

Following a liquidation and subsequent buy-out of the company by the Rickman brothers, the whole operation was sold to Lomax in 1992.

Rotrax

Dennis Adams' return to the British specialist car world after a spell in America was marked by the Adams Roadster, a fabulous, almost gothically styled roadster, initially sold only in complete form.

Adams' kit car project for the 1980s was the Rotrax, a sort of grown-up Tonka toy intended for the growing off-road recreational vehicle market. Launched in 1988, its chunky styling and immense structural strength appealed to a broad public. It used the greasy parts from a Cortina. While Adams sold the Rotrax himself — the first time he had actually run his own kit car company — a separate company offered a Land Rover-based 4x4 version, called the Dakar.

Respectable sales enabled Adams to invest in the development of a long-wheelbase four-seater Rotrax. In the 1991 recession, however, sales plummeted and he was forced to sell the project on to JS Specialist Vehicles after 85 examples had been produced.

Sylva

Sylva Autokits was one of the new generation of fun-oriented roadster kit firms to rival Dutton. The Sylva Star (1982) successfully used Vauxhall Viva/Chevette bits in a spaceframe chassis clothed in sharply-styled GRP and steel body panels. Priced competitively at £1,175, it offered far better quality than most of its competitors. Ford, Fiat and Alfa Romeo options followed.

The revised version of 1984, named the Leader, featured all-GRP bodywork. Only 70 of each model had been sold when their designer, Jeremy Phillips, decided to start from scratch again. The Leader was sold to Swindon Sports Cars in 1985 and was made by them until 1990 when it went on to Robley Motors for a short period.

In 1986 Phillips launched the back-to-basics Striker to a tremendous response. Thanks to its light spaceframe chassis, into which mostly Escort parts were fitted, the Striker scored several competition successes. Alternative engines included Mazda, Triumph, MG, Fiat,Peugeot and BMW. Next came the enclosed Clubman's Mk4, again principally Escort based, intended mainly for racing and sold through Phoenix Sports Cars of Daventry. Combined production of Strikers and Clubman's amounted to more than 200.

New for 1992 was the Fury, with enclosed bodywork similar to the Clubman's. An all-new chassis with specially designed suspension and Escort parts provided sharp handling and greater refinement.

Above: *The Rotrax, a sort of giant Tonka toy, was Dennis Adams' first kit car project following his return to the British scene from America.*

Below: *The Sylva Striker was the most basic and workmanlike of a series of competition-orientated sports kits from Sylva.*

Above: *Classic racing lines, blistering performance and superb engineering combined to make the 1986 Ronart W152 one of the most enjoyable road cars of recent years.*

Right: *The Regis Mohawk (1989) was one of the more convincing attempts at a kit-form sports coupé.*

Ronart

Arthur Wolstenholme's superb Ronart W152 was perhaps the purest and most powerful fun car of the decade. Its minimalist styling, inspired by the Formula 1 greats of the 1950s, and its thunderous Jaguar power made it an imposingly impractical conveyance.

Launched in 1986, the Ronart used a Spyder backbone spaceframe chassis with a choice of either aluminium or GRP bodywork. XJ6 or XJ12 engines could be fitted, and one Ronart was even sold with a bored-out Lister seven-litre V12 for shattering performance. For the less hardy, a full windscreen and hood could cover the otherwise massively exposed cockpit.

Expensive but beautifully finished, the W152 was one of the all-time greats of the kit car world. To date, about 25 have been made.

Regis

The first product of Regis Automotive was the RAM 4S of 1985, a blatant copy of the Lotus Elite 501 using, of all things, Cortina parts. A redesign was mandatory, and in 1989 the completely revised Regis Mohawk was launched. Retaining its Cortina basis, the new design was a fairly neat hatchback affair offering four full seats. A Rover V8 version was optional.

Next page
The CC Zero of 1991 marked a return to the fun car idiom.

CC

You can stumble across rusting Fiat 126s anywhere. The use of the little Italian engine in a fun car package was far from new, but Car Craft's Zero (1991) looked good and worked well. Its GRP and aluminium body fitted over a simple steel tube chassis and the whole kit cost £1,485. Buyers of the Zero were rewarded with open motoring pleasure on a shoestring budget.

Chapter Eight

Specialists of the 1980s

The 1980s and early 1990s have witnessed a tremendous diversification among British specialists, together with a significant leap in the quality of their offerings.

It is difficult to point to trends in a field which ranges from 50cc microcars right up to the most expensive cars ever made; but the revival fever apparent in the kit car industry in the 1980s struck just as hard in the more up-market limited-production arena.

The AC Cobra, Ford GT40, Jensen Interceptor, Reliant Scimitar GTE and Aston Martin DB4 Zagato all went back into production as official models, continuations of lines which had been broken for as long as 30 years. To some, this development smacked a little of kitsch, but the quality of the new offerings was irreproachable. To the companies sanctioned to produce these revivals (the term 'replica' was shunned), their commitment to them made strong commercial sense, as the value of the originals was often upwards of ten times the cost of building an entirely new car. And, in most cases, their efforts were rewarded with considerable success.

Also in vogue was 'retro-styling', usually some vague pastiche of pre-war design trends. Panther was the principal culprit, with the Kallista. Others included the Adams Roadster, Swift, Atlantis, Desande and Naylor TF; while still other manufacturers revived names of yore, such as Invicta, Lea-Francis and Railton.

But seekers of originality had no need to feel disappointed. The decade also witnessed the unequivocal return of the sports car. Not some pallid tin box with a GTi engine and spoilers, but the *real* sports car: the roofless two-seater with immense personal appeal, little practicality and a rasping exhaust note. In the wake of the Japanese (by now the acknowledged masters of the genre), a rich and exciting variety of such cars took to the roads.

This was the decade which saw Caterham Cars develop blistering versions of its Super Seven, Gordon Murray design the fun-and-thrills Rocket, Marcos re-establish itself with a revitalised range, and Ginetta launch the G33. On the periphery, there was a throng of minor hopefuls, among them the Harrier LR9, Gold Cirrus, Clan Clover, Tripos and Mirach.

In the second half of the decade, a peculiar new form emerged, apparently to cater to drivers dissatisfied with the performance of their Lamborghini Countachs and Ferrari Testarossas. The 'hypercar' or '200mph club' was a frankly bizarre collection of mostly European thunderwagons, extravagantly priced and boasting ever-spiralling top speeds, up to and beyond 250mph.

The Porsche 959 was probably the first such car. But there were British contenders, too, in this rarefied atmosphere: BRM, Schuppan, McLaren and Safir all claimed to have 200mph cars on their price-lists; others, like Costin and March, bowed out before realising their plans. Even Jaguar, with its XJ220, and TWR, with its JaguarSport XJR15, competed in this arena of madness.

Not that the expressionist 1980s escaped the tribulations which all specialist eras encounter. The decade began with Panther in receivership and ended with Reliant in the same boat. AC staggered on (what's new?) with various prototypes, none of which ever threatened to come to fruition. Lynx, Naylor, Middlebridge, Rapport and Glenfrome all experienced bankruptcy.

In the early years of the 1990s, there is no denying the diversity and optimism of the specialist fraternity. They continue to offer products for which, simply by virtue of their individuality, there will always be a demand. Moreover, the majority of those products are in an altogether different league from what was offered in the often slapdash era of their infancy — though that is not to denigrate those pioneer designers and builders whose efforts formed the foundations on which succeeding eras have built. Today, just as with the kit car industry, it is difficult to conceive of circumstances under which the urge to create and sell these fascinating vehicles could be extinguished.

Below: *The Argyll was something of an oddity: a four-seat mid-engined coupé with a very long wheelbase.*

Argyll

Whatever the Scots may pride themselves on, their motor car industry surely does not rate high. There was, however, one concerted effort to change all that: the Argyll.

Bob Henderson ran a Lochgilphead-based company called Minnow Fish, famous both for its carburettors and for being Europe's first manufacturer of turbochargers. His avowed intention was to build an all-Scottish supercar, which he did in 1975. Completed early the following year, Henderson's Argyll Turbo, as it was called, seemed set to take the sports car world by storm.

But delays in getting the tooling set up, then difficulties with the sub-contractor engaged in finishing and trimming the car, meant that the entire project was put on hold for no less than seven years until its launch in 1983. Not until July of the next year was the first car delivered.

The basis of the Argyll was a box section/tubular steel chassis. Among several scarcely-believable claims made by the Argyll Motor Company was that it was 'the most robust car ever made'. The all-GRP body enclosed the chassis and it was averred that the Argyll would easily last 30 years.

The production version's standard engine was the Peugeot 2664cc V6, coupled with a Minnow Fish turbo to give a top speed of 140mph. With the optional turbocharged Rover V8 in place, a top speed of 163mph was claimed. Unusually, these engines were mounted amidships in a body designed to accept four passengers (2+2, at any rate). Consequently, the car had a 9ft 10in wheelbase, so the ride was good. But Argyll tried to have it both ways, announcing that the handling was 'entirely neutral in all conditions' — quite a claim!

The styling, designed by engineers, was quite hideous. With a coat of rose-coloured paint, people could easily have mistaken it for the Pink Panthermobile. And, priced at £29,000 (some £10,000 more than a Lotus Esprit Turbo), the Argyll's only selling-point was that it was Scottish.

However, it did find custom. Its most popular market was, improbably, the United States where in later years Argylls were offered with four-litre racing derived engines. Even today, some 17 years after the car was first seen, you can still buy an Argyll.

Above: *Graham Nearn of Caterham Cars stands beside the Super Seven in the firm's Dartford factory.*

Caterham

Graham Nearn's Caterham Cars, an agent for the Lotus Seven, kept the stark two-seater alive after Lotus had abandoned production in 1973. Throughout the 1970s it marketed first the S4 and then the S3 Lotus Seven as the Caterham Super Seven, with a few changes and a choice of Lotus twin-cam or Ford 1600GT engines. The law said that the Seven had to be sold in kit form and Caterham chose to offer it only in complete component packages.

In the 1980s the Caterham became progressively more refined, adding more standard equipment and softer damping through the fitment of a Morris Ital rear axle. The choice of engines reverted to the 1600GT and the Sprint with its better cams, Holbay inlet manifold and Weber carbs.

Regular improvements followed, such as the 1983 long-cockpit model. Concerned that it was losing sales to cheaper kits (as indeed it was), in 1984 Caterham brought back the basic kit at a price of just £2,242; complete, it cost £6,500. By now Caterham had sold about 1200 Sevens and its popularity was still growing.

A Ford Sierra-based de Dion rear end became optional in 1985, and in 1986 the Seven scaled new performance heights with a bored-out 1691cc 'Super Sprint' engine with 135bhp on tap. Hardly had the dust

Above: *Luxury abounded in the very low-production Jaguar-based Rapport Forte of 1980.*

settled when Caterham launched its Cosworth BDR-engined Sevens, in 1600 and 1700 guise: power outputs were 150 and 170bhp and 0-60mph times were 5.3 and 4.9 seconds respectively. Caterham insisted that potential purchasers of the HPC, as it was christened, pass a special driving test before being permitted to buy one!

Then came the special-edition 'Prisoner', which capitalised on the fact that a Lotus Seven had been featured in the 1960s cult TV series of that name.

With production of the Cosworth BDR coming to an end, Caterham introduced a new HPC using the two-litre 16V Vauxhall Astra engine. Then its budget engine became the Rover Metro 'K' series 1.4-litre unit.

In 1992 came the scorchingly fast JPE (so named because of its endorsement by racing driver Jonathan Palmer). Its 250bhp engine was capable of taking this most advanced Seven from 0 to 60mph in just 3.5 seconds. Its cost? £34,950.

The current range consists of the 1.4, 1.6 Sprint, 1.7 Super Sprint, two-litre HPC and a new stripped-out Ford-engined entry model, the GTS. Over 4,000 Caterhams have been produced to date.

Rapport

In 1979, designer Chris Humberstone joined forces with Rapport International, whose trade was modifying Range Rovers, mostly for Arab customers. The first fruit of this merger was the Rapport Forte of 1980.

With wedgy styling by Humberstone, the Forte was a four-seater with an electrically-operated steel and aluminium roof which folded into the boot. Its body was also of steel and aluminium, with GRP wings, and its mechanical basis was the Jaguar XJ12. With the 5.3-litre V12 fitted, it sold for £36,774 (less with a smaller XJ6 engine). Its price reflected the Forte's luxurious leather-and-suede interior, air-conditioning and other appointments.

In 1982, however, the company's ambitions were wrecked by the arrival of the receivers. At least one estate model had been built, along with just a few convertibles. Alongside modified Range Rovers and drophead conversions, Rapport had also made the Ritz, at the same time. This was basically a Honda Accord (!), spruced up with a restyled glassfibre bonnet, boot, front wings, spoiler, rear skirt and a curious bar which acted as a headlamp cover, plus some luxury touches inside. Available with or without turbocharger, only 40 or so were made.

Triking

Draughtsman and Morgan trike fanatic Tony Divey built his own updated version of the Morgan in 1978. So much interest was shown that a year later he decided to put his vehicle, named the Triking, into production.

A strong backbone chassis with a steel spaceframe carried stressed alloy and some GRP body panels. Wishbone coil spring/damper front suspension was supplemented by a single rear wheel suspended on a swinging fork and driven by a shaft from an exposed Moto Guzzi Vee-Twin engine. The standard 844cc 68bhp engine endowed the 7cwt car with sizzling performance, but the tuned Le Mans and 950cc 71bhp engines were shattering: 121mph and 0-60mph in 7.8 seconds for the latter. Fabulous handling and a delightful five-speed Moto Guzzi gearbox made the driving experience exciting, if unrefined.

The cost was £4,500 complete, though from 1981 buyers were able to buy the Triking more cheaply in kit form; a hood and even automatic transmission were later options. The 100th Triking was built early in 1992.

Above and below:
Bringing back memories of the Morgan Super Sports: the lively motorcycle-engined Triking three-wheeler.

DeLorean

The John Z. DeLorean story is quite an epic. The vast sums of money invested by the British Government in his sports car project led to full-scale investigations, with enormous media coverage, and are still the subject of court proceedings.

An ex-General Motors high flyer, DeLorean touted his idea for a dramatic but high-volume sports car around several countries, in the search for financial support. The British Government took the bait, offering grants and loans totalling more than £80 million if DeLorean would set up shop in economically-struggling Northern Ireland. 'Of course I will,' was the American's unsurprising response.

The ingredients of the DeLorean DMC-12 should have led to success: a chassis engineered by Lotus, a body styled by Giugiaro and a V6 engine from the Peugeot/Renault factory. Nor, given that it was to be built exclusively for the American market, was there anything wrong with its projected price of $25,000.

But somehow the reality was different: the brushed steel bodywork attracted dirt and scratches like chalk; the gullwing doors often leaked and, it was rumoured, could trap the car's occupants in a crash; the quality of the early cars, built by an inexperienced workforce, was such that a second factory had to be opened in Los Angeles to rebuild them; and the rear-mounted engine gave indifferent handling. Despite massive production targets, only 8,800 cars were built between the car's launch in 1980 and the collapse of the DeLorean Motor Company in 1982.

The financial irregularities which subsequently came to light, causing the re-intervention of the British government, have been documented in copious and confusing detail elsewhere and are not really the concern of this book. Suffice it to say that the Delorean is now something of a cult car, with varying opinions about it still frequently expressed.

Above: *Brushed steel and gullwings doors were not enough to save the DeLorean from a financially turbulent demise*

Opposite page
Above, right: *The Panther that almost never was: the mid-engined Solo lasted just one year in production.*

Bottom: *Based on Panther's Lima, the Kallista was heavily re-engineered but lacked the quality and finish of the older car.*

Panther

When Robert Jankel's Panther Westwinds went to the wall in December 1979, it looked like the end of the line. But a buyer emerged in the form of Korean industrialist and car enthusiast, Young C. Kim, whose company Jindo Industries purchased Panther in 1980.

Kim inherited a few unfinished J72s and De Villes which were built up and sold on. In 1981 a budget version of the Lima with a Vauxhall 1800 engine was introduced alongside the 2.3-litre model. In the same year a revised J72, called the Brooklands, was also introduced, but only five were sold.

Jankel, who had been retained by the new Panther Car Company as a consultant, helped on the development of its new model, the Kallista. (He left before it was completed to concentrate on his Le Marquis marque and Robert Jankel Design.) The Kallista was basically a simplified but enlarged Lima. Its aluminium body panels (in place of the Lima's glassfibre) were made in Korea and shipped over to Byfleet, Surrey, to be assembled into complete cars.

Its engines came from Ford: the 96bhp XR3 unit gave it a top speed of 105mph, while the 135bhp 2.8-litre Granada engine brought it closer to 120mph. With cheaper manufacturing costs and lower equipment levels, Panther was able to sell the Kallista for less than the Lima had cost — from £5,850 at its launch in 1982. 200 were sold in just a few months, boding well for the company's future.

While the Kallista plugged away through the 1980s (latterly with the new 2.9-litre Granada engine), it was haunted by Panther's 'shadow' model, the Solo. It all but remained a shadow, too. When first shown in 1984, the Solo was to be a cheap Ford Sierra-powered mid-engined two-seater. Its Heffernan and Greenley-styled body looked good, but the arrival, in the same year, of Toyota's MR2 upstaged it and Panther finally decided to push the Solo up-market.

When the Solo re-appeared five years later, it had a two-litre Cosworth engine, Ferguson four-wheel drive, ABS and a revised Kevlar composite body which, to most eyes, looked far fussier than the original. Business opened in 1990, but the car was given a mixed reception: although it was an excellent handler, its ride was poor and its build-quality questionable — faults which on a £40,000 sports car should have been ironed out before production. The Solo was withdrawn from sale in June 1991, after just 12 had been delivered.

Exactly one year earlier, production of the Kallista had ceased (total production 1,672), so Panther became a car company without a car to sell. The parent company subsequently announced that it would resume Kallista production in Korea, bringing the British side of the Panther story to a rather sad ending. Korean-built Kallistas are scheduled to be relaunched in Europe in 1993.

Left: *Described as an 'all-terrain sports car', the Glenfrome Profile of 1985 was marketed almost exclusively in Arab countries.*

Below: *The very fine Atlantis drew on the pre-war Delage for its styling influences.*

Glenfrome

Glenfrome was one of a number of firms engaged in converting Range Rovers into mini-palaces with six doors, six wheels and so on. In 1975 it had built the Delta, a two-door Triumph Dolomite Sprint mid-engined sports car, which never went into production.

In 1981 the company asked ex-Marcos stylist Dennis Adams to create a sort of Arab-buggy on a Range Rover basis. The Glenfrome Facet was the result, a rather grotesque 4x4 machine, positively dripping with leather, walnut and electrical buttons. Typically, these vehicles were sold to Middle East customers for sums in excess of £50,000.

The model was pepped-up in 1985 with the launch of the restyled Profile, but Glenfrome failed the following year. No better luck attended Elektiar's subsequent revival of the Profile.

Atlantis

The genial Michael Booth's ambition was to design, build and sell his own car — a dream which he fulfilled in style with the Atlantis A1. This magnificent Jaguar XJ-based tourer, exquisitely built and finely proportioned in the style of Figoni, was completed in 1982.

Booth offered replicas of his four-seater at £39,000, but demand was slow and, after making only half-a-dozen, he opted to sell the Atlantis in various kit-form stages. Remarkably, an example was raced with some success in the Kit Car Racing Series.

The beautiful drophead version which arrived in 1985 brought no increase in demand, and the Atlantis disappeared quietly with very few cars sold.

Above: *Formula One styles infiltrated the bizarre Cartel TIGER.*

Cartel

A firm better known for its body-styling kits, Cartel briefly essayed car manufacture with the TIGER of 1983. The name was an acronym for Turbo Inter-cooled Ground Effect Roadster and was coined by the car's instigator, Chris Humberstone.

The TIGER's dramatic shape was inspired by racing car principles — it was claimed that Ken Tyrrell assisted with its ground effect technology — while the forward-hingeing canopy was a definite Humberstone quirk.

With a Renault 2664cc V6 mounted amidships, claimed performance was 140mph and 0-60mph in under six seconds, or even better if the optional twin turbos were ordered.

The intention was to make the rolling chassis in Britain and have the remainder completed in the USA — the TIGER's principal market — at a rate of 200 a year. Prices were to be low (from £8,000), but Cartel decided that its interests were best served by sticking to its flourishing bodykit business and the TIGER roared no more.

Swift

The idea of one man creating a car from scratch to compete with the likes of Morgan and Panther may seem recklessly optimistic. In the event, John Swift's attempt to do it proved to be exactly that; but he gave it a darned good try.

The Swift KJ280, launched in 1983, was of a high standard in all respects. On its backbone steel chassis was fitted a fabulous aluminium body (built by the same man who formed most of the early Panther J72 bodies). A Ford Granada 2.8-litre engine took care of the donkey-work. Inside the cabin, there was plenty of luxury and fine materials.

But at £12,500 for a complete component-form package, the Swift was expensive; nor did it have the prestige and access to publicity to do battle with its established rivals. Few, if any, were sold.

Above: *The Swift KJ280 of 1983 ought to have vied with Panther and Morgan, but in the event proved a commercial flop.*

Safir

Safir Engineering got the blessing of both Ford and JW Automotive Engineering to build what is called the GT40 MkV in 1981. As such, it was the first — and only — true replica of the Ford GT40.

Safir continued its chassis numbers in direct sequence from the last of the originals; and its specification, with only minor changes to the chassis, suspension and brakes, was virtually identical. Sold as the 'real thing', it wore a price-tag of £50,000.

It took a few years to get (very limited) production rolling, with a variety of Ford V8 engine options. With the 390bhp 4572cc Weslake engine in place, Safir claimed that the MkV would reach 200mph. Just 40 examples were planned, most of which have now been built. The last few are of lightweight aluminium monocoque construction and are priced at £188,000.

Below: *A 'genuine' Ford GT40: the Safir GT40 continued production of the monocoque Ford GT40 for the 1990s.*

Cursor

Alan Hatswell's Replicar Ltd., purveyors of kit-form replicas of Bugattis, Jaguars and Ferraris, launched its 'revolutionary micro vehicle' in 1985. And a decidedly strange beast it was.

Called the Cursor, it was a single-seat three-wheeler whose main selling-point was that it was classed as a moped and could therefore be driven by 16 year-olds. Its extremely odd-looking glassfibre body sat on top of a tubular steel chassis. Cryptically described as a 'GT hatchback convertible', it boasted nothing more sporting than a 49cc Suzuki moped engine; presumably the GT tag derived from the fact that it was mid-mounted. A top speed of 30mph was offset by fuel consumption of about 90mpg, and all for £1,724.

Replicar claimed grandly that 'the impact on driving will be much the same as when the Mini was launched in the late 1950s'. In fact, drivers (even of the 16 year-old variety) stayed away in droves. Its chances cannot have been helped by the appearance at the London Motorfair of a Cursor covered in gold metal-flake paint!

Right: *A strange fish, the Cursor: a single-seater 49cc microcar with gullwing doors and the air of a fairground dodgem*

Naylor

Naylor Bros was an established MG restoration company which latched on to the popularity of nostalgia-mobiles and launched its own replica of the MG TF in 1985.

It was actually quite a well-done replica, with steel panels hung on an ash frame. It could even be said to revive the MG tradition of putting Morris components in a sports car body: the front suspension, rear axle, engine and gearbox all came from the Morris Ital. Quality was high, but performance wasn't (95mph tops) and its price of £12,500 was higher than that of a restored original TF.

In 1986 Naylor went under, but the venture was rescued by restorer Maurice Hutson who relaunched the car as the Hutson TF and offered kit-form versions under the name Mahcon TF. The price for the complete car increased over the years (by 1991 it was £19,000) and at the time of writing the Hutson is still available.

Bamby

Alan Evans' attempt to re-invent the bubble car in the 1980s was quite credible, strange as that might seem. A microcar enthusiast, Evans was inspired by the Peel P50 (see Chapter Four), and in 1983 his first Bamby made its bow.

Like the Peel, the Bamby was a single-seater glassfibre-bodied three-wheeler with a 49cc engine. It weighed all of 235lbs and could do 100mpg. And it looked pretty good, too, although its price of £1,597 was decidedly on the high side.

Soon some design changes were made: the single gullwing door was changed to a conventional door, and the air vents, which had let a wasp into one customer's car, were blocked off with a kitchen sieve.

An initial production rate of 20 per month proved over-optimistic and the Bamby died after a year or so. The unsold bodyshells were reportedly sold to a Midlands firm to use as paddle-boats on its lake!

Below: *1987, and Prime Minister Margaret Thatcher throws caution to the winds in a Naylor TF 1700.*

Right: *1983 Bamby: a tiny single-seater three-wheeler which aimed to revive the bubble car.*

Below: *A new chapter at Ginetta. Under new management, the model line-up in 1990 (from left to right): the relaunched G12, the G32 convertible, and the Rover V8-powered G33.*

Ginetta

The waxing and waning fortunes of Ginetta Cars since its birth in 1957 eventually overtook the four Walklett brothers, who had run the company through thick and thin. In 1989, deciding that retirement was overdue, they finally sold Britain's oldest surviving kit car firm to a northern consortium, which took over the firm's recently-acquired base in Scunthorpe.

The new owners decided to put the existing Ginetta model, the G32, through Type Approval and so sell it complete. This marked the end of Ginetta's kit car activities. Now it could compete with the car it was always intended to out-handle, Toyota's MR2; and, at a price of £10,945, it significantly undersold it.

Based around Fiesta XR2 mechanicals (from which model it also took its doors), the G32 was a mid-engined GRP two-seater offering a top speed of 128mph and a 0-60mph time of 7.9 seconds. An optional 135bhp 1905cc engine did even better. From 1990, there was also a convertible version.

Ginetta's important newcomer, also in 1990, was the G33, engineered by Ivor Walklett (the only brother to stay on in the new regime) and styled by his son, Mark. It was based on the G27, but sported twin head fairings, new pop-up lights and an angular windscreen surround. Under the body were Ford Sierra Cosworth independent suspension all round and Rover V8 power — a first for Ginetta. Two versions were offered: the 145bhp 3.5-litre and the 200bhp 3.9-litre, the latter reaching 129mph and 0-60mph in 6.7 seconds. It was stark, brash and unrefined, but a joy to drive fast.

Two classic Ginetta models were also re-introduced by the new management, initially for export only: most went to car-hungry Japan. The original G4 was relaunched in both open and closed form, while the gorgeous G12 mid-engined racer of 1966 was revived for the road at an export price of some £50,000.

But Ginetta was a victim of the early 1990s recession and suffered two liquidations in 1992, the second only weeks after a Motor Show appearance with two new models, the 1.8-litre Ford-engined Club and the bored-out Rover V8-powered SC Roadster, with numerous styling and specification changes over the G33. At the time of writing, a further rescue bid looks probable.

Above: *The Ginetta G32 coupé was the first of Ginetta's new era of Type Approved sports cars.*

Left: *What do you get if you strip down a Bentley Turbo R and build your own two-door body for £600,000? The Hooper Empress.*

Hooper Empress

Before the advent of the new Bentley Continental R, Rolls-Royce was without a modern two-door car (the Corniche dated from the late 1960s). The coach-builder Hooper & Co. was the ideal candidate to do the honours, offering both a two-door Bentley Turbo R and the much more ambitious Empress.

First seen at the 1987 Geneva Motor Show, the Empress was a stupendously opulent means of getting from A to B. The Bentley Turbo R on which it was based was entirely stripped before being built up again with two-door bodywork featuring all-new styling — which in fact was hardly very graceful. Individual customers were able to specify exactly what sort of leather, wood and other little exclusive touches they desired, but in return for the privilege they could count on having to fork out more money than for any other car then available: no less than a whopping £275,000.

Hooper embarked on a stately production rate of three cars per year. The Empress, still on its list at time of writing, can now be purchased for the altogether reasonable sum of £600,000.

Chapter Nine

The Outer Limits – or "Were they Serious?"

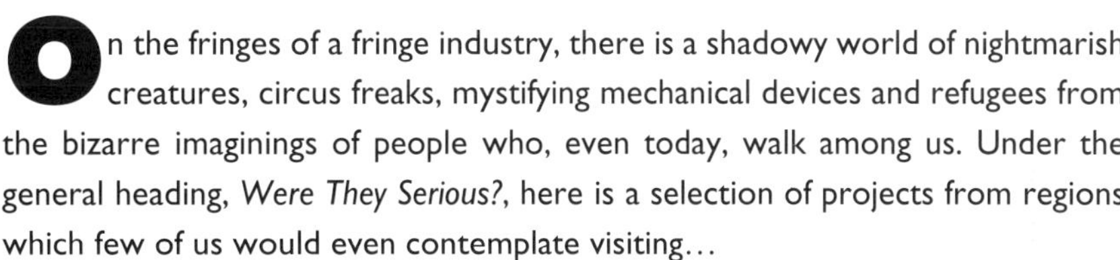

On the fringes of a fringe industry, there is a shadowy world of nightmarish creatures, circus freaks, mystifying mechanical devices and refugees from the bizarre imaginings of people who, even today, walk among us. Under the general heading, *Were They Serious?*, here is a selection of projects from regions which few of us would even contemplate visiting…

Wolfrace Sonic

Champion special builder and street rod king Nick Butler (later to launch his own production car, the Gold Cirrus) had already embarked on creating a science-fiction roadgoing machine when Barry Treacy of Wolfrace Wheels heard about it. Wanting a publicity replacement for his six-wheeled Range Rover to attract interest in the new Sonic wheel, he approached Butler with an offer of sponsorship to turn it into an even more extravagant six-wheeler.

The result, the Wolfrace Sonic, was completed in 1983. This was no mock-up over a Beetle chassis: it had a seamless steel tube chassis, a stupendously swoopy body, electrically operated opening cockpit, six wheels shod with Pirelli P7s, and two computer-controlled Rover V8 engines working in parallel through twin Borg Warner automatic gearboxes. It actually drove, too, and Butler claimed that the combined engines' output of 400bhp would take the seven-litre Sonic to 150mph.

Never intended for production (as if...), it was, Butler admitted, a temperamental beast. 'It's a toy, really, not even a Sunday car. It's a once-a-month job, and then you spend the rest of the month putting it back on the road again.'

Quasar-Unipower

Quite why Universal Power Drives, manufacturers of the lovely Unipower GT, got involved with as whacky a project as the Quasar-Unipower is an absolute mystery.

In 1968, Vietnamese-born fashion designer Quasar Khanh designed a bold new vehicle which he persuaded UPD to build. Yet the element of design was conspicuous mainly by its absence — for where is the stylist's hand in the creation of a transparent mobile cube?

A strong tubular steel chassis contained widened Mini subframes, with a Mini Clubman engine sited beneath the rear passengers' bottoms. Glassfibre panels covered the chassis, while a substantial steel tube frame rose up to hold huge sheets of toughened glass in place. Entry was via sliding patio doors at either side (or on some versions through the front) and the four passengers sat on transparent plastic seats, ensuring that absolutely everything was on show. A green-tinted roof struggled to prevent the interior becoming a greenhouse.

Shorter than it was wide and narrower than it was high (5ft 4in by 5ft 6in by 6ft 2in), the little cube was a dreadful car to drive — unless you were obsessed, to the exclusion of all else, by good visibility. It was flat out at 50mph; not that you'd want to go at that speed in a vehicle which promised shattering shards of glass in your face at the slightest incident.

Six Quasar-Unipowers were built by UPD during 1968. What became of these exhibitionists' delights is transparently unclear.

Previous page
Nick Butler's one-off twin-engined Wolfrace Sonic was sponsored by a wheel manufacturer. Realistically, Butler never envisaged a production run.

Left: *Ice-cube-on-wheels Quasar-Unipower really did work... for those prepared to face the hazards of driving one.*

Outspan Orange

By a strange coincidence, Outspan commissioned the building of six machines almost diametrically opposed to the Quasar-Unipower. The Oranges, made during the early 1970s, were conceived purely and simply as advertising gimmicks. Mini parts were fitted in a specially-made chassis, over which a spherical glassfibre Orange was proudly placed. Entry to the cockpit was via a rear door and the occupants arranged themselves on seats facing into the centre of the Orange, where the driver sat. Orange-tinted glass completed the picture. The three Oranges which survived are currently being restored to be put back into service!

Sinclair C5

Sir Clive Sinclair should surely have known better. His infamous Sinclair C5, which he financed from his own pocket, was an unmitigated disaster and all but sunk him as an entrepreneur.

The C5 cost only £399 and could be driven legally by 14 year-olds. It was also a truly environment-friendly vehicle, its battery-and-pedal power offering a range of up to 20 miles. The trouble was, it was not exactly driver-friendly. The hapless C5 owner had to sit exposed to the elements, to exhaust fumes and, worst of all, to advancing juggernauts, with his hands fumbling under his buttocks attempting to steer it. And he had to pedal up hills, as the battery couldn't cope.

Sinclair aimed to produce no less than 100,000 C5s from a Hoover factory within the first year. But things got off to a prophetically bad start when it snowed heavily on launch day, in January 1985, and the C5 turned into a toboggan. By February, several local authorities had banned its use amid well-founded fears about driver safety.

In April, production halted due to 'a gearbox fault', but it quickly became obvious that disastrously poor sales were the real reason for the stoppage. Sinclair put the project up for sale in June, found no buyer, and so left the receiver to pick up the pieces in October. Only a few thousand had been supplied.

***Above:** Publicity wagon. Six Outspan Oranges were commissioned during the early 1970s; three survive and are currently being restored for re-service.*

***Right:** One of the great commercial disasters of modern times, the Sinclair C5 was intended to reach a six-figure production total, but achieved less than ten percent of that target.*

Above: *Bill Carter's G-Whiz brought Top Gun to the streets. Measuring 21 feet, it had a claimed top speed of 150mph, with a 0-60mph time of 7.9 seconds and fuel consumption of 11mpg.*

G-Whiz

Street rod builder Bill Carter got bored with the genre (who could blame him?) and decided to create 'something totally different'. Over the next two years to 1987, his labours bore fruit in the form of a 21-foot-long aircraft with wheels.

G-Whiz was styled around a Hawk fighter 'plane canopy which Carter was lucky enough to acquire and convincingly mimicked the shape of a 'plane. Using Jaguar XJ12 parts in a simple chassis of Carter's own design, it actually drove very well, as Carter proved when he travelled 16,000 miles in it visiting shows.

There were plenty of clever touches. The 'fighter pilot' steering control was a cut-down Allegro 'Quartic' wheel, the petrol tanks were twin chromed ten-gallon beer barrels, the front suspension could be raised to clear obstacles, and the heater/demister was a hair-dryer. The two passengers sat in tandem.

Carter sold G-Whiz to finance a second road-going 'plane based around a Buccaneer screen. Completed in 1991, it was rather more practical, and painted in shocking pink!

Jephcott Micro

The Jephcott Micro was the 1984 brainchild of engineer Dr. Jephcott. It pioneered the use of technology which made the car lean into bends and, with a body designed by Richard Oakes, it looked for a while as if the project would proceed further. As it was, it simply faded away, although it was displayed for nine weeks at the London Design Centre.

Bond Bug Four-Wheeler

This extraordinary device consisted of two Bond Bugs, stuck together back-to-back. Why would anyone want to do this? Simply because it was the only means by which Bond could get to display the Bug at the British Motor Show, where SMMT regulations prohibited three-wheelers from being exhibited. This way, the Bug qualified as a four-wheeler. Tom Karen of Ogle Design, who hatched the idea for and designed the Bug, remembers: 'It caused some consternation at the show, not least with me. I hated the thing.'

The only other four-wheeled Bug was a prototype constructed by Bond with the wheels in their conventional locations, but the car was never productionised. However, a firm called WMC resurrected the Bug in 1990, with a choice of three or four wheels.

Right: *The Jephcott Micro: 1984 'lean machine' which might have become a production car but faded into obscurity.*

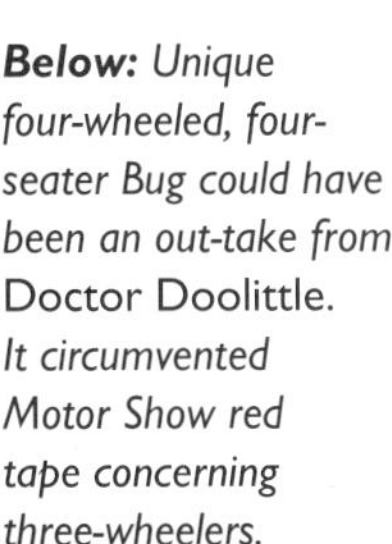

Below: *Unique four-wheeled, four-seater Bug could have been an out-take from* Doctor Doolittle. *It circumvented Motor Show red tape concerning three-wheelers.*

***Above:** Quest. Wanda Ventham, on set for the TV series* UFO, *ponders on the possibility that this vehicle was seriously intended for a production run.*

Quest

The story of the Quest is surely one of the most preposterous and improbable tales ever told.

Once upon a time, there was a man called Gerry Anderson, creator of the marionette heroes of *Thunderbirds*, *Stingray* and others. In 1968 he directed a film called *Doppelgänger* and met up with racing car builder Alan Mann, whose sideline was film prop manufacture (which had included *Chitty-Chitty-Bang-Bang*). Mann was contracted to build three suitably space-age vehicles for the film, to a design penned by Derek Meddings.

Space-age it might have seemed in 1968, but in retrospect it just looks plain ugly. Under the body lurked nothing more advanced than a Ford Zephyr chassis powered by a Cortina GT engine. The fakery extended inside the car, with a profusion of nuclear-drive switches and lights, none of which actually did anything and whose effect was rather lessened by the Mk2 Cortina instruments.

However, while the car was being filmed on location it was spied by a chap called Sidney Carlton who subsequently persuaded a tycoon friend, David Lowes, to invest in putting the vehicle into production. The Explorer Motor Company was formed and £25,000 was spent on development, including making glassfibre moulds. The plan was to buy new Zephyrs from Ford and plonk the glassfibre shells on them. The resulting four-seater vehicle was to be called the Quest.

To attract potential buyers (who would have to stump up £3,000), a couple of additional gimmicks were thrown in: fibre-optic cables connected from the lights to the dash-board to reassure the driver that they were all working; and a 'guaranteed harmless' radio-active gas-filled fascia to provide 24-hour illumination.

In 1970, everything suddenly went quiet and the Quest died. Except that it didn't quite die. Both Quest prototypes were bought by Pinewood Studios for use in its magnificently mediocre TV series, *UFO*, where they were piloted by the likes of Commander Straker, Colonel Foster, and Wanda Ventham, until filming tragically ceased in 1973. UFO2 ended up in the hands of DJ Dave Lee Travis in 1975.

Two of the three cars still exist and are owned by film enthusiasts. As to the fate of the third, it is either lurking undiscovered in some dark alley-way or has returned from whence it came, somewhere beyond the outer limits...

PART TWO

A-Z Directory

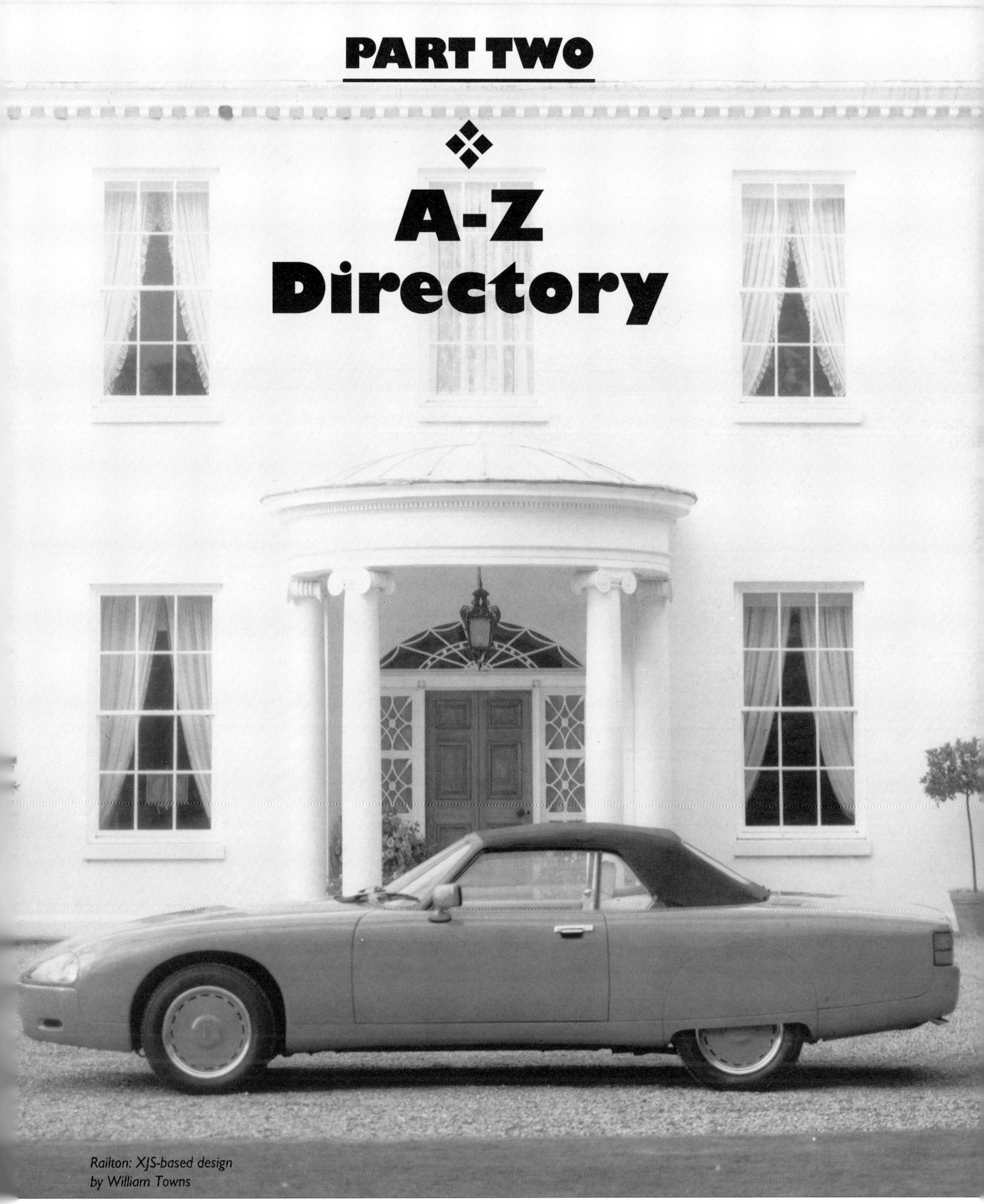

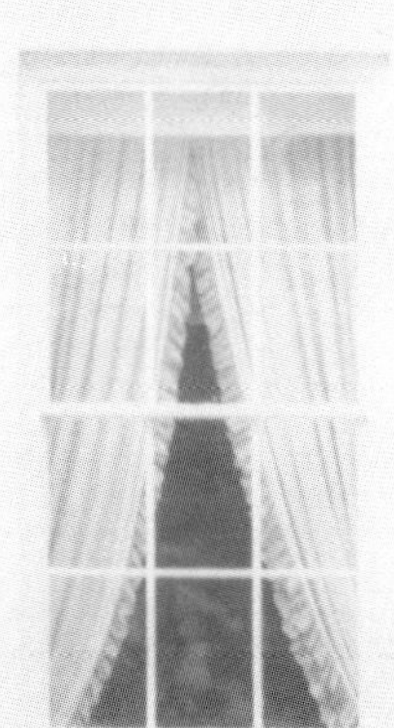

Railton: XJS-based design by William Towns

Above: *1958 Allard Palm Beach II*

Left: *1985 Alto Duo*

Below: *1971 Anglebug*

A-Z Directory of Postwar British Specialist Cars

NAMES which have been treated at greater length in Part One show relevant chapter numbers in bold type.
Where PRODUCTION DATES have been impossible to verify, they are either omitted or queried.
In cases where cars have been known by ALTERNATIVE NAMES, they are cross-referenced.

ABI. See AF 1971-80.
ABC 1971. Glassfibre three-wheeler with replica Mini front end and Mini power.
ABS 1988-91. Countach replica called the Scorpion, developed from Broadbest Primo (qv). Also, from 1990, an open version, the Monaco.
AC 1910-date. Famed British firm, latterly for Cobra and 428. Fortunes waned in 1970s when ME3000 mid-engined sports car took five years to reach production. Project passed to AC (Scotland) in 1984, which replaced it with the Ecosse (1985) — assumed by Ecosse Cars (qv). Original AC showed front-drive Ford-based Ace in 1986 and Autokraft (qv) were to make it. Unhappy Ford involvement from 1987 scotched the Ace project, but Ford sold out to Angliss' Autokraft in 1992, allowing a revised Ace a chance to enter production.
AC 1983. Curious metal-bodied Mini-based three-wheeler, the AC Donington.
AC 1992-date. A Countach replica.
ACM 1981-83. Importers, then exclusive manufacturers, of the German Fiberfab Bonito, a Beetle-based GT40-ish sports coupé. Passed on to AED (qv), then to Seraph (qv).
AD 1982-86. Questionable kit car maker first known as Perry Automotive Developments. Models: Karma — Beetle-based Ferrari Dino 'lookalike', taken on by RW (qv); 400 — a four-seat open sports car based on the Karma and later sold as the Chimera by Trident Autovet (qv); Spirit SS — a gross Mercedes SS100 'replica', went to Spirit (qv); and 427 — a poor Cobra replica. AD also made chassis and bodies for the Gravetti Cobra (qv).
ADAMS 1986-date. Noted stylist Dennis Adams (Marcos, Probe) designed his own Roadster, a flamboyant retro-sports car based around the Jaguar XJ6. Also the Rotrax. **(7)**
ADD. See Nova.
ADJ 1989. Three models: Cobra 427 and GT40 replicas, plus Jaguar-based Merlin roadster.
ADT. See MacIntosh.
AED 1983-84. Took over the Bonito from ACM (qv), adding front-engined chassis and convertible versions. Seraph (qv) bought it after AED's bankruptcy.
AEM. See TMC.

Above: *1970 Arkley SS*
Left: *1984 ASD Minim*

Opposite page
Top: *1978 Aston Martin Bulldog*
Below: *1988 Autotune Gemini*

AF 1971-80. Pretty Mini-based three-wheelers. **(5)**
AF 1987-89. Superior '30s-style kit, the AF Sports, using variety of engines including Fiat and Toyota in a space-frame chassis.
AFRICAR. Laudable 'world car' attempt of late 1980s. 4x4, 6x6 or even 8x8; 4,8 or 12 gears; Citroen 2CV, Subaru and even specially-designed engines from 38 to 300bhp; wooden body/chassis. Too ambitious.
AG 1992-date. Spitfire/Herald-based traditional roadster.
AIMS. See Fergus.
AK 1992-date. Cobra replica dubbed the KF 427.
AKS. Pretty 1950s GRP shells with the name Continental in MkI (open), Mk2 (hardtop) and Mk3 (2+2 coupé) forms.
ALBANY 1971-81. Fine Edwardian-style vehicular carriages. **(6)**
ALEAT 1991-date. Amateurish sheet-steel sports kit for Jaguar power.
ALEXIS 1961 and on. Noted racing firm which made a few trials specials and chassis for GRP shells in the early 1960s.
ALLARD 1937-60. Legendary sports/trials manufacturer. Few of any type made. Models: K1/L1/J1/M/P/J2/K2/J2X/ M2X/P2/Safari/K3/Palm Beach/J2R/Clipper/Palm Beach II.
ALLORA 1986-date. Lancia Stratos replica with Beta mechanicals, inferior to Transformer (qv). Project revived as Litton Corse, then Carson Corse.
ALTA 1931-54. Formula 2 racing firm, produced 2-litre saloon after WWII.
ALTO. See Peerhouse.
ALTO 1985-88(?). Brave attempt at Mini-based city car with modern design.
AMICA 1980. Beetle-based Mercedes SSK 'replica', initially sold as the Delta.
AMPLAS 1984. Took on Embeesea (qv) Eurocco, by then called SN1. Also a Porsche 911-inspired convertible called the Pulsar. Project assumed by Lemazone (qv).
ANDERSEN 1985-date. A Moke lookalike called the Mini Cub.
ANGLEBUG 1971-72. First and only attempt at a Ford Anglia-based beach buggy. Front engine made it look ridiculous.
ANNE'S BUGGIES. Obscure buggy shell manufacturer.

APOLLO 1971-72. Beetle-based Chevron Can-Am-inspired exotic kit with gullwing doors. Never reached planned production.
AQUARIUS 1971-72. Standard beach buggy fare.
ARGYLE 1991-date. Revival of the Berkeley (qv) T60.
ARGYLL 1976-date. Curious mid-engined Scottish sports car. **(8)**
ARKLEY 1970-date. Successful body conversion for MG Midget with fun/traditional cross-over flavour. From 1985 with new manufacturer. Several hundred supplied.
ARNOTT 1951-57. Sports cars made in small series by designer Daphne Arnott.
ARROW. See EG.
ARTEESI. Authentic-style steel bodies for Austin 7 chassis, available from late '70s.
ASD 1984-date. Bob Egginton's design involvement in numerous kit car projects (Tripos, GE, Maelstrom) extended to his own marque, ASD. Models: Minim (mid-engined Mini-based open two-seater); Hobo (Mini-based utility); a Maserati 250F replica; and imports of the Canadian Allard J2X replica.
ASHLEY 1954-62. Supplier of shells and chassis. **(2)**
ASQUITH 1982-date. Maker of 'antique' commercial vehicles on Escort and Transit chassis; also presented a retro-style taxi and limousine.
ASQUITH 1987-date. Makers of the Vista MHP MkI (using original pre-war Riley parts) and the MkII (on modern Ford parts).
ASTON MARTIN 1922-date. World-renowned sports car maker. Three unusual projects of recent years: the Ogle prototype of 1972 **(6)**; the Bulldog (1978), a William Towns-designed mid-engined gullwing supercar claimed to exceed 200mph; and the Sanction 2 (1991), a series of four replicas of the original 1960 DB4 GT Zagato, the idea for which was hatched when the firm realised there were four unused chassis numbers from the original production run.
ASTRA 1956-60. Initially called the Jarc Little Horse, this 322cc micro station wagon was sold fully-built or in kit form. Few were made.

ASTRON 1984-85. Brick-like open kit car with Cortina mechanicals.
ATLANTIS 1982-90(?). Attractive Jaguar-based nostalgia cars. **(8)**
AURIGA 1992-date. New manufacturers of Noble (qv) 23.
AUTECH. Faithful 1980s C-Type Jaguar replica in aluminium.
AUTOBODIES. Two-seater GRP coupé shells of 1950s in Mk1 and Mk2 forms.
AUTOBARN. See Gecko.
AUTOCULT. See Tigress.
AUTOKRAFT 1980-date. The only firm licensed to make a Cobra replica with the name AC Cobra. Continued Cobra production with the MkIV. High quality, high cost, high performance in later cars.
AUTOTUNE 1984-date. Based success on popular Jaguar XK120-ish Aristocat. Revived Marcos Mantis in 1986 as the Mirage. Gemini was an open Cortina-based kit on a 1950s Falcon (qv) shell. XK140 fixed-head replica arrived in 1991, and M1 Racer in 1992.
AVA 1986-87/1990-91. Modern-looking and aerodynamic (Cd = 0.295) kit called the AVA K1, with front-mounted Ford power. Revived in 1990.
AVALON 1990-date. Strikingly styled mid-engined Escort-based kit, originally called the Curtana.

THE ENGINE TUNER

MARIO di CAPITE

Rolling Road Tuning

Optimum performance and fuel economy whatever you drive!

You don't drive your car at idling speed, so the only 100% way of tuning and diagnosing problems is in our rolling road tuning bay at road or race driving speeds. Telephone now for details.

- Standard & performance car servicing
- All makes of carburettor tuned and serviced
- Fuel injection and turbo specialists
- Race car preparation & engine building

DELLORTO CARBURETTORS AGENT

VISA

Unit 10, The Adam Business Centre,
Cranes Farm Road, Basildon, Essex
(0268) 280862/726749

Tyne Bridge Autocentre

THE NORTH EAST'S KIT CAR BUILDERS

- Full or part builds undertaken
- High standard of paint finishing
- Accident repairs to classic and prestige cars

6, The Arch, Brandling Street, Gateshead,
Tyne & Wear NE8 2BA
(091) 478 4041

VEHICLES

MOTOR COMPANY LTD

The Rickman range of open top, eycatching fun sports cars, available in 3 or 4 wheel form,easy to build using Citroen 2 or 4 cylinder mechanical, and even simpler to insure.

The range of LOMAX — utility styled vehicles, are highly practical, with Ford mechanicals, robust galvanized chassis; and colour impregnated G.R.P. body shell. Available in saloon, convertible and van guides, with seating from 4 to 7 in comfort. also available the highly acclaimed Rancher 2 berth motorhome.

ENDURANCE WORKS,
MAYPOLE FIELDS, CRADLEY,
WEST MIDLANDS B63 2QB
TEL: 0384 410910 - FAX:0384 69574

LE MANS D TYPE

CHASSIS BODY KIT ONLY £2495.00 + *VAT*

THIS KIT CAN BE COMPLETED
AND ON THE ROAD IN ONLY 10 DAYS

Call, Write or Phone
LE MANS SPORTS CARS LTD
110 HOUNSLOW ROAD — WHITTON — MIDDLESEX TW2 7HB
TEL: 081 894 5937

KOUGAR ©

KOUGAR SPORTS MKII MKIII

Jaguar Based Kit

Based on a body style from a previous era, the Kougar Sports incorporates all the advanced engineering of the XJ Saloon. This comprehensive kit can be assembled in 40-50hrs with 3.4 or 4.2 engine options & choice of 80 gel-coat colours. Send for brochure.

P.M. STREET AUTOMOTIVE ENGINEER
HARBINS•TRENT•SHERBORNE•DORSET DT9 4SU•ENGLAND
TEL: 0935 850667 FAX: 0935 850068

TIM WALKER (RESTORATIONS)

Aylesbury, Buckinghamshire

We service, repair and restore veteran, vintage, pre-war and early postwar cars.
We have carried out major and minor work on Alvis, Aston Martin, Armstrong, Avon, Austin, Bentley, Bristol, Daimler, Ford, Hillman, Humber, Jowett, Lagonda, Lanchester, Lancia, Lea Francis, MG, Morris, Mercedes, Riley, Standard, Singer, Sunbeam Talbot, Triumph, Vauxhall & Wolseley.

NEW! To enable your funds to stretch further, we also offer a 'selective restoration service'. We dismantle individual components, strip them completely, you collect and clean and paint as guided and we repair, rebuild and fit.

We run a budget account system, and we like to have owners visiting to see progress.
If you think we can help, please ring.

Tel: Aylesbury 0296 770596 workshop 0296 748419 home

AVANTE 1982-86. Handsome Beetle-based two-seat sports coupé, also offered with Golf GTi power. Approximately 30 produced.
AVIA 1961. 2+2 GRP coupé on Herald chassis which never reached production.
AWE 1990-date. GRP tub with 'traditional' styling for Herald/Spitfire chassis.

B

BADSEY 1978. Bill Badsey emigrated to South Africa before productionising his Eagle targa, based on the BMC 1100. There he made the Bullet which UVA (qv) were to sell in the UK in 1982.
BAJA 1971-date. Original buggy style, now made by GT Mouldings (qv).
BAMBY 1983-84. Single-seat microcar. **(8)**
BARNARD. F6 racing constructor which tried, but failed, to productionise a vintage Mercer replica in 1972.
BEACH BUGGIES 1971-72. Guess what this firm made?
BEAMAN. Rather plain Jaguar MkIX-based tourer. Production: 6.
BEAUFORD 1985-date. Ingenious, beautiful and successful tourer. **(7)**
BEAUFORT. Mid-1980s Austin Ruby-based roadster kit.
BEAUJANGLE 1971-73. After offering a cheap T-bucket hot rod kit, Beaujangle launched the Can-Am, a US-designed fun car only 36ins high based on a shortened VW chassis. Production: 5. Briefly revived in 1985 by Lemazone (qv).
BEAVER 1984-85(?)/1991. Uninspiring Escort-based estate kit styled by Richard Oakes.
BEDOUIN. See CVC.
BENZ. Early 1980s Model A Ford tourer replica, plus period vans. Mercedes-Benz objected to the use of the name.
BERKELEY 1956-61. Attractive Lawrie Bond-designed sports microcar. **(2)**
BILMAR 1971. Lotus Seven-style device called the Buccaneer. Production: 13.

***Right:** 1986 Avante*

***Below:** 1986 AVA K1*

***Bottom:** 1971 Baja GT*

BIOTA 1968-76. Originally-styled Mini-based sports two-seater: fast and fun. Production: 31. The planned Mod (Mini-based utility) never materialised.
BIRCHALL. See McCoy.
BIRCHFIELD 1985-87. Fabulous all-metal interpretation of the Jaguar SS100. **(7)**
BJS 1987. The Mistral was a horrid 2+2 gullwing kit using Cortina bits.
BM 1971-72. Another GP-based beach buggy available in long and short wheelbase versions.
BOHANNA STABLES 1972-78. The Diablo was going to be the Mk2 Unipower (qv) but was completed with BL Maxi 1500 power. Design sold to AC (qv) which modified it to become the ME3000. The Nymph of 1975 was an Imp-engined fun-buggy. Production: 34.
BOLER 1971-74. Tasteless Model T fun bucket. Production: 30.
BOND 1949-75. Micro manufacturer extraordinaire, headed by Lawrie Bond. Models: MkA/MkB/MkC/MkD/MkE/MkF/MkG/875/Equipe/Equipe GT4S/Equipe 2-litre/Bug.

BONGLASS. Early specials era GRP shell.
BONITO. See Seraph.
BOUILLOT-HELSEL 1983. Sumptuous Jersey-based replica of the Jaguar E-Type. Ridiculously expensive.
BOXER 1986-87. Poor quality mid-engined Mini sports car designed by Ian Shearer, creator of the Nimbus (qv).
BRA 1981-date. UK's first 289 Cobra replica. **(7)**
BRADLEY 1990-date. Modern spaceframe with old Ashley (qv) shell, called the S61.
BRIGHTWHEEL 1986-89. Sheldonhurst (qv) Cobra revived as the Viper. Also a Countach replica called the CR6 Stinger. Taken over by Cobretti (qv).
BRITANNIA 1957-61. Tojeiro-designed GT sports car with Ford Zephyr engine. Too expensive. Production: 6.
BRITON. See Kestrel.
BROADBEST 1987-88. The Primo was a Countach replica taken over from GTD (qv).
BROOKE 1991-date. Tandem two-seater with Renault 5 engine, in the style of a 1950s Vanwall racer.
BROOKES 1956. Ex-Singer engineer's GRP shell for Ford chassis.
BROOKS 1951-52. Small Austin Seven-based roadster.
B&S. See EWM.
BUCKLAND 1985-date. Delightful GRP three-wheeler, the B3, with Ford 1300cc engine and Morganesque styling. About 1 car made each year.
BUCKLER 1947-62. Leading chassis maker, usually fitted with contemporary GRP bodies. Buckler made its own alloy body and a Galt Glass GRP shell. The MkV and 90 models were factory-built. Production: 500 chassis.
BUGATTI 1981. Mysterious usurper of the name — a Type 35 replica which appeared at Motorfair in 1981.
BUGLE 1970-72/1979-85(?). Original-looking beach buggy made to an American design in short and long wheelbase versions. 800 made during buggy boom. Revived by CW Autos, then GT Mouldings (qv).
BULLOCK 1972-73. Ugly by name, ugly by nature: an awkward Ford Anglia-based open sports car, offered as the B1, then B2 with Herald front suspension. Production: approximately 35.
BURLINGTON 1980-date. First model, the SS, was a blatant Morgan copy on a Spitfire or own chassis, which was sold to Dorian (qv). Pioneered a range of plans-built cars: the very successful Arrow and Berretta '30s-style roadsters, the Chieftain jeep and the Centurion, all for Triumph chassis.
BUROCHE. Typical GRP shell of the late '50s and early '60s.
BUTTERFIELD 1961-63. The Butterfield Musketeer was a bulbous GRP two-seater GT and one of the first kits to use Mini parts.

Above: *1985 Lemazone Beaujangle Can-Am*
Below: *1975 Bohanna Stables Nymph*
Bottom: *1986 Brightwheel Viper*

CALVY 1983-date. MGB-based 1930s tourer too close to the NG (qv) for comfort, so redesigned. Turbulent history but moderately popular.
CAMBER 1966-69. Designed by Derek Bishop of Heron (qv) and George Holmes, the Camber GT was an unusual-looking Mini-based two- or 2+2 seater. Production: 6. Resurfaced under new sponsors as the Maya GT. Production: 6.
CAMBRIDGE. 1950s aluminium-on-ash body for Austin 7 chassis.
CAPRICORN 1985. Jeep-style kit for Mini parts.
CARIBBEAN 1981-83. Designed by ex-Reliant chief engineer, a Reliant Kitten-based GRP car intended for tourist resorts. Models: Cub/Cob.
CARISMA 1990-92. The Carisma Century was a Ford-based SS100 lookalike.
CARLTON 1983-date. The Commando was a big Cortina-based estate, low on quality but also on price, so sold well. Sporting Carrera (1985) had a choice of Cortina, Rover V8 or Jaguar power. Took over the MC Acer (qv) in 1989, but its planned De Tomaso Pantera lookalike, the Montana, never reached production.
CARSON. See Allora.
CARTEL 1983-84. Abortive attempt at a stunning sports car. **(8)**
CARTUNE 1971-72. Buggy of Belgian origin (Apal). *Custom Car:* 'Stylistically not the greatest thing since smokey bacon crisps.' Project assumed by Magenta (qv).
CATERHAM 1973-date. Authorised maker of Lotus Seven after Lotus abandoned production. **(8)**
CAVALLO 1983-85. Attractive four-seat convertible, the Estivo, not so attractively using BMC 1100/1300 parts. Sold as a kit but withdrawn so that it could be developed as a complete car. It never came back.
CC 1991-date. Amusing little Fiat 126-based fun car. **(7)**
CENTAUR. See Concept.
CHALLENGER. See Triple C.
CHARGER/CHEPEKO. See Embeesea.

CHEETAH 1983-86. Quite possibly the worst quality kits ever made. From the Mirach of 1983 through the Shamal, SV1, 427 Cobra, GT40 and Miura, there was hardly a glimmer of integrity. Few sales.
CHESIL SPEEDSTERS. See Street Beetle.
CHEVRON 1961-date. Famous racing constructor dabbled with a roadgoing GT in 1966 but only seven were made. In 1990 the B16 racer (last made in 1969) was revived for the road in the form of the B16R. Chevron also put its name to a roadgoing replica of the B8, launched in 1992, made by Scott Ellis Racing (qv).
CHILTON. Early 1980s Bugatti Type 35 replica with Beetle power.
CHURCH GREEN ENGINEERING. See Gozzy.
CIPHER. See Stevens.
CITY MOBIL. See Jephcott.
CK 1989-date. The Gravetti/GE (qv) Cobra revived.
CLAN 1971-74. Novel Imp-based sports two-seater called the Crusader. **(6)**

Top: *1968 Maya GT*
Above: *1985 Carlton Carrera*

CLAN 1983-87. Restyled Clan (qv) made in Northern Ireland. In 1986 the rather more serious Alfasud-engined Clan Clover emerged, albeit briefly.
CLASSIC AUTOMOTIVE REPRODUCTIONS 1983-84. A company offering to build any car the customer required. It built an 'approximate' Mercedes SSK replica, a Countach and the imported Contemporary Cobra.
CLASSIC CARS OF COVENTRY 1980-84(?). One of the makers of the Viking (qv). Also made the Mercedes 320 'staff cars' for the film *Raiders Of The Lost Ark*, replicas of which were offered for sale in 1983, ironically based on the Jaguar MkIX.
CLASSIC ERA. Early '90s maker of aluminium C- and D-Type replicas.

CLASSIC IMAGES 1992-date. Two models: the AWR '30s-style roadster and the MSR3 Renault 5-based three-wheeler.

CLASSIC REPLICARS. See Western Classics.

CLASSIC REPRODUCTIONS. See Sandwood.

CLASSIC ROADSTERS 1991-date. An accurate Austin-Healey 100 replica (Sebring MX) and a flared-arch Chevrolet-engined Healey (MX Lightning).

CLASSIC SPORTS CARS 1987-89. Datsun 240/260Z-based Ferrari GTO replica.

CN 1985-date. Lotus dealer offering a slightly modified kit of the Elan named the Sprint.

COBRA 1970-71. Nothing to do with AC, just another GP buggy rip-off.

COBRETTI 1990-date. Revival of the Brightwheel Viper (qv), sold as the Viper 4, V8 and V12, reflecting the engine options available.

COLDWELL 1967-69. Attempt to make a road/race GT with mid-mounted Mini power. Production: 6.

CONAN 1986-88(?). This Countach replica had possibly the worst name ever given to a car — the Conan Terminator.

CONCEPT 1973-77. Probe (qv) adapted with Imp engine for kit run, first with Perspex gullwing doors, then with conventional doors and 2+2 option. The Condor roadster was never properly launched. Project passed to Pulsar (qv).

CONCORD. TR2-style GRP shell of the 1950s.

CONNAUGHT 1947-57. Interesting open sports cars which spawned a successful F1 car. Models: L2/L3. Total production: 16.

CONVAIR. Low-slung glassfibre shell of 1950s.

COOPER 1948-69. Primarily a racing concern, but some road cars were made between 1948 and 1952, either with Cooper's minimal aluminium body or as one-offs.

COPYCATS 1982-date. Deservedly one of the top names in replication. Copycats offered a C-Type replica with an aluminium body for Jaguar Mk2 parts or a GRP version for XJ6 parts, in kit form or

complete. There were also a beautiful aluminium or GRP D-type replica, an XKSS replica and, in 1992, a copy of the Jaguar XJ13 one-off. The firm changed its name to Proteus in the late '80s.

CORNISH CLASSIC CARS 1985-86. Two models: the Parisienne, a 2CV-based Edwardian four-seater rather like the Siva (qv); and the Osprey, a VW-based Mercedes SSK replica.

CORONET 1957-60. Practical 328cc open GRP three-wheeler. Production: approx. 250.

CORRY 1983-84. Davrian (qv) heavily restyled by Cipher stylist Tony Stevens (qv) as the ugly Cultra. Brief production run in Ulster.

COSTIN 1970-72. Marcos (qv) founder Frank Costin's Amigo was an ambitious Vauxhall VX 4/90-based GT. Fast and with masses of integrity, it was too expensive. Production: 9.

COUNTESS. See Kingfisher Mouldings.

COUNTRY VOLKS. See FF.

COVIN 1984-date. Porsche 911 replica called the Turbo Coupé, modified after Porsche objected. A cabriolet followed and in 1989 a Porsche Speedster replica for VW Variant parts was added. Its 1986 McLaren M6 replica was stillborn. DJ (qv) relaunched the Covin range in 1992.

COX. See GTM.

CRAYFORD. Well-known cabrio-conversion firm which imported, then made, the Argocat off-road/amphibious vehicle from 1970.

CRS 1960-61. Box section chassis for Ford E93A parts and contemporary bodyshells.

CS+2. See Stimson.

CSC 1953-55. Two models: a 650cc lightweight sports car and a Rochdale-bodied Austin A30-based sports design.

CTR 1971-72. Straight copy of the Manta Ray (qv) beach buggy.

CURTANA. See Avalon.

CVC 1985-87(?). Basic utility vehicle, the Bedouin, on 2CV/Dyane chassis.

CW AUTOS. See Bugle.

CYBERTECH 1992-date. Yet another Countach replica.

CYGNET 1984-85. A classic of non-styling, the Cortina-based Cygnet Monaco 2+2 coupé was also of very poor quality. Amazingly, several were sold, though Cygnet's 'trad' roadster and Cygnetina roadster remained unique.

This page
***Top:** 1985 Covin*
***Above:** 1985 CVC Bedouin*
***Right:** 1984 Cygnet Monaco*

Opposite page
***Top:** 1975 Concept Centaur*
***Above:** 1985 Cheetah Cobra*
***Bottom:** 1986 Clan Clover*

DAKAR. See Adams.
DANTE. Alloy bodies of 1950s for Austin 7 chassis. Models: basic Sprint and flared-wing Clubman.
DARRIAN 1986-date. Rebirth of the Davrian (qv) in Wales.
DART 1991-date. Pig's ear of a roadster for Marina parts.
DASH 1989-date. Final version of the Pelland Sports (qv), first produced by Listair (qv), then Dash Sportscars, which also took over the MCA (qv) and turned it into an open-top.
DAVRIAN 1967-83. Fine-handling competition-orientated sports cars. **(5)**
DAX. See DJ.
DAYTONA CLASSICS 1986-87. Spirit (qv) modified and revived as the Gatsby, plus the ex-AD 400 (qv) — now the Magnum — a Cobra 427 replica and the 204GT, a Dino look-alike.
DE BEERS 1986. Fully-built GRP replicas of MG TD and AC Cobra on Nissan Sunny and 300 Cedric bases respectively.
DE BRUYNE 1968. Gordon-Keeble revived alongside a mid-engined coupé. **(4)**
DEEP SANDERSON 1960-69. Chris Lawrence's Mini-based coupé. **(3)**
DEETYPE 1974-date. Restorer Bryan Wingfield's superlative C- and D-Type replicas on Jaguar E-Type parts. Also Lightweight E-Type, XKSS and XJ13 replicas.
DELKIT 1984-85. Odd Cortina-based coupé kit called the Camino. Only a few were made.
DELLOW 1949-59. Trials manufacturer *par excellence*, mostly with Ford engines. Kits and, later, complete cars. Models: MkI/MkII/MkIIC/MkIIE/MkIII/MkIV/MkV/MkVI. Total production: approximately 300.
DE LOREAN 1980-82. Controversy from start to finish. **(8)**
DELTA. 1950s GRP shell whose instigator, Evans, went on to make the Evans Scorpion (qv).
DELTA. See Amica.
DELTAYN 1985-90. The Proteus was Deltayn's first project, the body for which was derived from the AD400 (qv). The Richard Oakes-designed Pegasus followed, then emigrated to France.

***Above:** 1988 Deltayn Pegasus*

DEL TECH. See Foers.
DE NOVO 1986-date. De Novo Kits made the Hornet, the prototype of which was called the KNW.
DEON. See JH Classics.
DESANDE 1981-82. Chevrolet Impala-based neo-classic of an American formula, built by Grand Prix Metalcraft and sold for £50,000.
DEVILIN 1992-date. Mid-engined Renault V6-powered coupé called the Futura.
DG 1982-86(?). Chopper trike with Beetle power, called the Phoenix.
DGT. See JH Classics.
DIAL 1970-71. Low, mean but unbuildable mid-engined kit with gullwing doors and Ford engines, called the Buccaneer. Production: 20.
DINGBAT 1971-72. Whacky fun car based on Triumph Herald chassis and instigated by *Cars & Car Conversions* magazine.
DIVA 1963-66. First model, the GT, based on Heron (qv) shell. Production: 64. Followed by the mid-engined Demon prototype which became the Valkyr road/racer. Production: 5. Finally, the GT-based 10F of 1966. Production: 3.
DJ 1979-date. Prominent kit manufacturer which based its success on its Cobra replicas. **(7)**
DMS 1989-date. The Bullit allowed you to convert your Ford Capri into an Aston Martin Volante lookalike (!) Of more merit were the 1990 Abingdon (MGA replica) and the Venom (Cobra replica).
DNK. See De Novo.
DOLPHIN. 1950s special shell.
DOMINO 1986-date. Desirable Richard Oakes-styled open Mini fun car called the Pimlico; Premier had half-doors. The HT was a fully-enclosed version, essentially a GRP Mini. Domino also took over the Vincent (qv) Hurricane.
DORIAN 1986-88. The Burlington SS (qv) revived.
DOUGLAS TF 1990-date. Kit-form or fully-built replica of MG TF for Herald/Spitfire chassis or Ford basis.
DRAGONFLY 1981-86. Pretty sports car using MG Midget centre section as its basis. Resembled a scaled-down Panther Lima. Popular but lazily marketed.

DRAGONSNAKE 1990-date. Hand-built Cobra replica based on Dax (qv) but with wider rear wheel-arches. Price: over £36,000.
DRI-SLEEVE 1971-72. So called because a 'dry sleeve' protected the driver's arm when he used the external gear lever and handbrake, the Dri-Sleeve Moonraker was a fine Bugatti Type 35 replica in aluminium with GRP wings, plus a Cortina 1600GT engine. Fully-built or in kit form, it was exorbitantly priced. Production: 6.
DRK 1987-date. Trad-style three-wheeler for Renault 4/5 parts.
DUCHESS 1984. Roadster inspired by 1930s MG with aluminium-over-wood bodywork and Herald/Vitesse chassis.
DUNSMORE 1987-date. Fine hand-built open two-seater of '30s inspiration with Jaguar engine and fabric-covered wooden body.
DUROW 1985-date. Range of neo-classic extravaganza using MG Midget centre body swamped by outsize wings. Choice of GRP or stainless steel two- or four-seater bodies with names like Deluge, Starr and Debonair. Yum!
DUTTON 1970-90. Tim Dutton went from the humblest origins to become the world's biggest kit car firm and back again. **(5,7)**
DWORNIK. See Vincent.

E

EAGLE. See Badsey.
EAGLE 1981-date. Successful kit car firm with large range of kits. **(7)**
EB. At £39 for the shell, the EB50 must have been the cheapest kit car ever. Other 1950s shells were the 60 and the Debonair, also marketed in full kit form by LMB (qv).
ECO 2. Richard Oakes city car design of late '80s on Fiat Panda basis, with 'external' chassis.
ECOSSE 1988-90. Relaunch of the AC (Scotland) Ecosse with Fiat Croma two-litre turbo mid-mounted power, dubbed the Signature.
EG 1990-date. Ferrari Daytona Spyder replica, the Arrow, with Jaguar XJ12 engine.
ELAND MERES. See Rhino.
ELECTRACTION 1975-78. Attempt to manufacture electric cars in series. EVR-1 prototype became the Tropicana convertible but neither it, nor the Rickshaw, reached production.
ELEKTIAR. See Glenfrome.
ELSWICK. 1980s Mini-based car for disabled drivers, the Elswick Envoy, styled by William Towns.
ELVA 1958-68. One of the most respected specialist firms of its day. **(3,4)**
EMBEESEA 1975-84. The Siva (qv) Saluki redesigned as the Chepeko, then the Charger. Also the Eurocco. **(5,7)**
EMERY 1963-66. One of the first specialists to use a Hillman Imp engine (optional Ford 1050cc), the pretty Emery GT had a low GRP body over a spaceframe chassis. Production: 4.
ENCORE 1992-date. Beautiful replica of the 1957 Lotus Elite, using Ford parts.
ENFIELD 1969-76. Only successful UK attempt at electric car manufacture. The 8000 sold 106 examples, most to the Electricity Council. The Moke-style electric Runabout never made production. The Safari (1973) was an AMC Jeep-based 4x4 design in the style of the Range Rover.
ENGLISH CARS OF DISTINCTION. Late 1980s manufacturer of Jaguar-based replicas of the XK120, XK140, XK150 and E-Type.
ENTERPRISE 1983. Techno-pot luxury car with 4wd, turbo V8, ABS, Kevlar body — earmarked to cost £42,000, but the Enterprise F16 never even ran.
EPC 1970-72. Beach buggy with a touch of originality called the Hustler. Also an unusual-looking fun car, the Pinza GS.

ERA. Mid-1980s Bugatti Type 35 replica.

EUROCCO. See Embeesea.

EVANS 1979. Thwarted MG TF replica, the Scorpion, for Triumph Spitfire chassis.

EVANTE 1983-date. Vegantune's updated Elan steadily improved. Restyled 140TC in 1991. Firm was taken over by Fleur de Lys (qv) in late 1992 and specifications are currently (1993) being updated with Ford Zeta engine.

EWM 1984-85/1988-89. Dreadful Cortina-based roadsters called the Buccaneer and Brigand. Revived by B&S Sportscars as the Roadster and Sprint.

EXCALIBUR 1985-date. Evidently inspired by the Seraph Bonito (qv), initially on Beetle chassis, then with front-mounted Ford engines and, later, Rover V8. Convertible announced in 1992.

EXCELL. GRP shell of the specials era which seems to have been identical to the TWM (qv).

EXCELL. Bentley Mk6-based special of the early 1970s.

This page
Above: *1981 Elswick Envoy*
Below: *1991 Evante 140TC*

Opposite page
1987 Dunsmore

Left: 1955 Frazer Nash Le Mans Coupé

Opposite page
Top: *1991 Gold Cirrus*
Bottom: *1970 Grantura Yak*

F

FAIRLEY 1950. Five-seater convertible and two-seater road/race car with Jowett Javelin components.
FAIRLITE. The name under which Ginetta (qv) sold its G3 in bare kit form.
FAIRMAN CARRO 1991-date. Replica bodyshells of the Lotus Six and Eleven, the former intended for Ford Popular chassis as per the original.
FAIRTHORPE 1954-78. Long-lived British fringe manufacturer. **(3)**
FALCON 1958-64. Popular specials firm 'made good'. **(2)**
FALCON DESIGN 1983-date. Originally the kit manufacturer of the Stevens Cipher (qv), moved on to making the Lomax (qv), then its own models. **(7)**
FERGUS 1986-date. Fine Aston Martin Ulster replica for Morris Marina mechanicals. Sold fully-built or in kit form. Currently made by AIMS.
FES. See Kestrel.
FF 1981-date. Assumed the Rat (qv) buggy and designed its own range of buggies, latterly produced by Country Volks. **(5)**
FIELDBAY. See Magnum.
FIELDMOUSE 1971-72. Steel-bodied jeep for Ford Popular chassis.
FLETCHER 1966-67. Redesigned Ogle SX1000 (qv). Production: 4.
FLEUR DE LYS 1983-date. Maker of 1920s-style 'Newark' van range, offered the Landaulet from 1991 and subsequently the 'Lincoln' range of larger vehicles including 14-seater and 21-seater omnibuses.
FOERS 1977-date. Tough range of utility kits. **(7)**
FORCE 4 1991-date. Jaguar XJ-based replica of the Iso Grifo Mk1, dubbed the Bretsa.
FORMULA 27 1992-date. Yet another Lotus Seven lookalike.
FRAZER NASH 1924-57. Successful in competition, Frazer Nash road cars never really took off: only 78 of all types were made between 1948 and 1957. Models: High Speed/Le Mans Replica/Le Mans Replica MkII/Cabriolet/Fast Tourer/ Mille Miglia/Targa Florio/Le Mans Coupé/ Sebring/Continental GT.
FREE SPIRIT. See Hudson.
FRENETTE 1981-82. Moke Californian replica, unusually with a stainless steel body.
FRISKY 1957-64. Above-average microcar. **(2)**
FROGEYE 1986-date. Replica of the Austin-Healey 'Frogeye' Sprite. endorsed by Geoffrey Healey, using MG Midget engine.
FUNBUGGIES 1971-73. GRP replica of Bentley Speed Six, never properly launched.
FUTURA 1970-71. Ambitious GT design for Beetle chassis. **(5)**

G 

GALOPIN 1991-date. Fiat 126-based replica of Vignale Gamine 'Noddy car'.
GARDNER DOUGLAS. See GD.
GAZELLE. Infamous American replica of Mercedes SSK based on VW chassis and variously imported and made in Britain from 1979 as the Gazelle, Delta, Amica, Spirit, Osprey, Gatsby and Phoenix.
GB 1969-79. Blatant rip-off of the GP Buggy, the GB Buggy even sounded the same. It lasted until 1974. More original was the Invader buggy of 1971, taken from an American shell. Revived by GT Mouldings (qv) in 1987. Production: 150.
GB. Late 1980s maker of Reliant Fox-based van and convertible, the latter called the Raglan.
GB 1986-87. Early Countach replica: the GB500S.
GCS 1991-date. Straight Morgan copy in aluminium and GRP called the Hawke. Cortina parts.
GD 1990-date. A replica of the AC Cobra 427 Mk3 on a backbone chassis, originally known as the RW 427 (qv).
GDXM. See Griffin.
GE. See Gravetti.
GECKO 1984-date. Mini-based Moke-type kit with huge range of body styles and wheel configurations.
GEM. See Grantura.

GEMINI 1990-date. Lotus Elan lookalike with frogeye headlamps, improbably based on Vauxhall Chevette parts.
GENIE 1989-date. Scottish fun/ traditional cross-over kit car on Cortina bits, called the Wasp Clubman.
GENTRY. See RMB.
GILBERN 1959-76. Wales' foremost sports car manufacturer. **(3,6)**
GILCOLT 1972. Strange gullwing three-wheeler based on Reliant Regal chassis.
GILL 1958. Two-seater coupé version of the Astra (qv). A failure.
GINETTA 1957-92. UK's longest surviving kit car company, latterly moving up-market. **(3,7,8)**
GITANE 1962. Mid-mounted Mini power for this unusual GT coupé. Production: 6.
GLENAULD. See Helian.
GLENFROME 1975-86. Range Rover conversion experts turned manufacturers. **(8)**
GKN. Supercar designed to go from 0-100mph and back again in record time. **(6)**
GOLD 1991-date. Designed by ex-hot rod supremo Nick Butler, the Gold Cirrus was a Rover V8 mid-engined two-seater of unusual appearance.
GORDANO 1946-50. Advanced sports car with independent suspension and Cross rotary-valve engine. Production: 2.
GORDON-KEEBLE 1960-67. Highly-acclaimed GT which nearly succeeded. **(4)**
GOZZY 1978-83. Japanese-sponsored Mercedes SSK replica. Modern Mercedes 280 parts in a design engineered by ex-F1 ace Len Terry. Very accurate and beautifully made, justifying its £30,000 price tag. Only six were made before disenchantment from Japan.
GP 1967-date. Foremost beach buggy manufacturer, followed up with a succession of best-selling kits. **(5,7)**
GPB. See Teal.

GRAHAM AUTOS. See Ryder.
GRAND ILLUSIONS 1991-date. GRP Triumph TR2 replica.
GRANTURA 1968-73. TVR-like three-litre Ford V6 coupé, the Gem, followed by the Mini-based Moke-style Yak (production: 150).
GRAVETTI 1983-88. A dreadful Cobra replica, initially made by AD (qv), sold as a 'Cob in a box'. Taken over briefly by GE Cars before being assumed by Bob Egginton of ASD (qv), who had been charged with re-engineering the car. Renamed the CK (qv).
GRIFFIN 1975-85. This pretty dual-purpose convertible/estate began life as the GD-XM but soon became the Griffin. Based on Morris Minor parts, with a VW Beetle version arriving in 1978, it just faded slowly away, despite attempts to develop it further.
GRIFFON 1985-date. Looking dashed similar to the Merlin (qv), the Griffon 110 used Vauxhall Viva/Magnum parts.
GRINNALL 1992-date. The Scorpion 3 was a BMW K series 'bike-engined three-wheeler.
GROUP SIX 1972-77. VW-based boxy sports kit styled after Group 6 race cars, initially with open, then with coupé, bodywork.
GRS 1983-89. Ginetta's Hunter-based estate kit. **(7)**
GS 1975-80. William Towns' idea of how the Lotus Europa should look, offered as a conversion for Europas. Production: 15.
GSM 1961. South African-designed Delta. **(4)**
GTD 1985-date. Initially a KVA (qv) agent, GTD made its own spaceframe chassis and GT40 replica bodyshells in MkI and (from 1990) MkII styles. In 1987 came the fabulous Lola T70 replica, again with a spaceframe chassis and a choice of mid-mounted engines. GTD's Countach was taken on by Broadbest (qv).
GTM 1966-date. Excellent little Mini-engined sports cars. **(3)**
GT MOULDINGS 1982-date. Resting place for old buggies, including the Cartune Apal, Invader, Kyote, Kubel, Manta Ray, Bugle and Baja GT, the last of which was also available in long wheelbase form as the Sahara.
GUYSON 1974-77. This William Towns-designed slab used a Jaguar E-Type as its basis. Production: 2.

H

HACKER 1991-date. Dutton's return with the fully-built Hacker Maroc, a four-seat GRP convertible based on the Ford Fiesta.
HALDANE. The HD 100 was an Austin-Healey replica of the late '80s with a Ford or other four-cylinder engine.
HAMBLIN. Tiny Austin 7-based shells: the cycle-wing Cadet and the aluminium all-enveloping De Luxe.
HAMILTON 1991-date. Took on Dutton's Sierra, Shuttle and Beneto.
HAMPSHIRE CLASSICS. See Moss.
HARBRON 1986. Basic open roadster kit.
HARE ENGINEERING 1989-date. Another GT40 MKIII replica, the HE 40 MKIII used a spaceframe chassis.
HARRIER. See HMC.
HARRIER 1991-date. The LR9 was an Alfa Romeo 164 three-litre mid-engined targa sports car from a racing enterprise.
HAWK. See Wyvern.
HAWK 1991-date. A Cobra 289 replica developed by Gerry Hawkridge of Transformer (qv), followed by the Le Mans (hardtop 289), the 2.6, a six-cylinder version of the 289 with cut-down wheelarches, a Willment Le Mans Cobra replica, the V12, a 275GTB replica, and a 288GTO replica for racing only.
HAWKRIDGE DEVELOPMENTS 1992-date. Gerry Hawkridge's Transformer (qv) made under an alternative name.
HEALEY 1946-54. Donald Healey's own sports car marque. Models: Westland/Elliott/Sportsmobile/Silverstone/Tickford/Abbott Drophead Coupé/Nash-Healey/G Type. Total production: 1,125.
HEALEY. See HMC.
HEEREY. See GTM.
HELIAN 1983. Quite attractive Welsh roadster with Ford engine, Viva suspension and four-seat traditional body of aluminium, steel and glassfibre. Very few made.
HENSEN 1983-85. Hideous

Granada-based coupé, the M30 and M70; and a Cobra 427 replica. The M30 passed on to Eagle (qv).
HEPWORTH. Specials era shell.
HERITAGE ENGINEERING 1985-date. Jaguar-based replicas of C-Type and SS100 Jaguars; plus, from 1989, a Lister-Jaguar 'Knobbly' replica. In 1991 came a racing replica of the Lola T70 Spyder.
HERON 1959(?)-64. Pretty GRP hard or soft top shell, the 750, for Austin Seven chassis. Modified to become the Heron Europa of 1963 with Ford mechanicals. Too cheap for its spec. Production: 12. Made under licence in Switzerland as the MBM.
HERON 1986. Suzuki dealer's motorcycle-engined microcar prototype, the Tripod.
HG 1960. Obscure Welsh special.
HIGHLANDER. See Jimini.
HI-TECH 1987-90. Appalling GT40 replica, also available with removable roof.
HMC 1990-date. Based on the Harrier prototype, HMC offered an updated Austin-Healey 3000 concept with a Rover V8 engine in two forms: the MkIV and the Silverstone (the latter with less luxurious trim). Initially called the Healey (Geoffrey Healey was involved), but the holders of the name objected. High price and consequently slow sales.
HOME-BUILTS 1983-84. Plans-built Jeep for Mini van floorpan.
HOOPER. Celebrated coachbuilder made the Empress **(8)** from 1987.
HORNET. See De Novo.
HRG 1936-56. Manufacturer of Singer-based hand-built sports/trials/competition cars. Models: 1100/1500/1500 Aerodynamic Twin-Cam. Total postwar production: 201.
HUDSON 1990-date. Made the remarkable Free Spirit Renault 5-based single-seat three-wheeler, later joined by the tandem two-seater, Kindred Spirit and four-wheeled Mystic.
HUMBERSTONE. Two of Chris Humberstone's own designs were earmarked for production but never made it: the TTS Triplex six-seater and the Midi.

HURN. Early 1990s replica of the classic Lotus Elite, remarkably faithful.
HUSTLER 1978-89. William Towns' novel modular kit design. **(7)**
HUTSON 1986-date. The Naylor TF (qv) under new management. **(8)**
HWM 1950-56. Celebrated Formula 2 and sports-racing constructor which converted some of its race cars for the road.

Top: *1991 Hacker Maroc*
Middle: *1951 Healey Tickford*
Above: *Humberstone Midi*

Opposite page
1974 Group Six

I

IAD. Famous design house produced a replica of the Pegaso Z103 with Rover V8 power for a Spanish corporation in 1992.
IKENGA 1968-69. Extraordinary McLaren M6-based road car. **(4)**
IMPALA 1981-85. Boxy little Fiat 500-based fun car. **(7)**
IMPERIAL. See Minion.
IMPERIAL 1989-90. Gross American-designed neo-classic with the names Corsair and Royale.
INNES LEE. See Scorpion.
INTERSTYL. William Towns' design company offered several bodykits for contemporary cars and the Tracer of 1986, a Metro mid-engined GRP open two-seater, briefly sold in kit form. The Black Prince Reliant-based roadster of 1985 never reached production.
INVADER. See GB.
INVICTA 1946-50. Pre-war firm revived with the Black Prince four-door saloon and two-door convertible. Production: 25.
INVICTA 1982-84. Jaguar XJ6-based traditional car, the Tourer, plus a Jaguar XJ13 replica called the Tredecim, with Jaguar V12 power and a claimed top speed of 200mph.
INVICTA REPLICAS 1985. Another Cobra copy for Ford V6 power.
IOTA 1947-52. 500cc racing car builder and monocoque pioneer which made, in 1952, a 350cc road sports car.
ISS. See Kestrel.

J

JAG 1950-52/1954-56. Basic sports car based on Ford Pilot V8. Revived in 1954 as the RGS (qv) with Ford 1172cc or MG engines, in kit form. Production: 50.
JAGO 1965-date. Hot rod pioneer turned kit jeep maker. **(5)**
JAGUARSPORT 1989-date. Two 200mph+ supercar projects. The XJ220 began as a works special built in engineers' spare time. Much modified, it entered production in 1992 with a V6 3.5-litre twin-turbo engine and a price tag of over £400,000. TWR, with which Jaguar had a 50% stake in Jaguarsport, also started making the Group C-derived XJR-15 in 1992, even more expensive and probably faster.
JAYE. Accurate early 1980s Jaguar XK-based replica of C-Type Jaguar.
JBA 1982-date. Successful open sports kit maker. **(7)**
JBF 1992-date. 2CV-based three-wheeler in Morgan style, called the Boxer.
JBM 1946-51. Stark open roadster with modified Ford Pilot engine.
JC. See Wyvern.
JC 1984-89. John Cowperthwaite of Moss (qv) offered plans-built models under this name: the Herald-based Midge and Locust (Lotus 7 lookalike), both also available with a Ford-based chassis. Taken over by T&J Sportscars (qv). Also briefly made the old Moss range.
JEFFREY 1968-75. The J4 was a highly-praised but stark roadster kit on a racing chassis with a GRP and aluminium body. Production: 30. Replaced in 1972 by the J5, with more curvaceous bodywork. Production: 32.
JENARD 1955. Rakish sports special only 32ins high with choice of Austin, MG and Coventry-Climax engines.
JENSEN 1983-date. Revival of the Jensen Interceptor (last made in 1976). Revised in 1987 as the S4 with 5.9-litre Chrysler V8, also in 'notchback' form. Low production levels.
JH CLASSICS 1988-date. Producers of the DGT Ferrari Dino copy with Lancia components and later the option of Ford 2.9-litre V6 power. Also Scoperto (targa) and Le Mans (speedster) versions. In 1991 acquired the Noble P4 (qv) and renamed the marque Deon.
JIFFY. Richard Oakes-designed Mini-based van range of early 1980s.
JIMI JIMP 1981-84. Reliant Kitten-based fun/utility kit.
JIMINI 1973-date. Moke replica initially with aluminium body, later restyled and, in the 1980s, with GRP bodywork. Briefly known as the Highlander.
JOHNARD 1976-79(?). Bentley-based sports car, the Donington.
JPR 1985-date. Makers of the Wildcat E-Type lookalike, Cortina- and then later Jaguar-based. Also 2+2 and Le Mans coupé versions. Took over the Vanclee (qv) from Dutton (qv).
JS. See Adams.
JZR 1990-date. Entertaining Morgan-inspired three-wheeler with Honda 'bike engines.

***Left:** 1988 FES Briton (Kestrel)*

Opposite page
***Top:** 1986 Kingfisher Kustoms Kommando*
***Bottom:** 1983 Kingfisher Mouldings Countess*

K

KARA 1991-date. The KaRa 430 was a Ford RS200 Group B replica.
KARMA. See RW.
KAT 1989-date. Bodykit firm which offered the MPV, an Escort-based car with interchangeable GRP bodywork allowing up to ten body styles.
KD 1991-date. Cobra 289 replica on Cortina basis.
KELVEDON 1987. Replica of the Lotus 47.
KENLEY 1986. Squarish Herald-based roadster.
KENMAR. See Shirley.
KENNEDY. See Squire.
KESTREL 1984-87/1988-89. Well-made 1930s-style GRP roadster with one drawback — its VW floorpan. Later sold as the FES Briton.
KESTREL. See Scorpion.
KIEFT 1952-55. Racing car-based sports models.
KILLEEN. Tom Killeen built a whole string of specials from the 1950 K1 onwards. The first was a pioneer of monocoque design. The K18, an Imp-based coupé, was intended for production. It didn't make it, but formed the basis for the Scorpion (qv).
KILO 1983-84/1986. Squarish trad-style roadster on Morris Minor chassis.
KING 1970-71. Bizarre hot rod/fun car King Thing was Ford-based. Mike King went on to tailor-make one-offs to order.
KING. See Libra.
KINGFISHER 1982-84. Over-ambitious attempt to revive the Minijem (qv) as the Kingfisher Sprint; also in Turbo form. Failed revival in 1985 as the Vortex.
KINGFISHER KUSTOMS 1983-date. Several VW-based kits: the Kommando (sand rail); Kombat (beach buggy); Kango (sort of modern buggy); and imports of the American Chenowth off-road rail.
KINGFISHER MOULDINGS 1983-86. Singularly awful replicas of the Countach (Countess), Bugatti Type 57 (Vulcan) and Jaguar E-Type. More convincing Countach shell sold to GB (qv).

KITDEAL. See Noble.
KOUGAR 1977-date. Brutally stark but beautiful Sports is Frazer Nash-like Jaguar-based doorless sports car, still in production. The Monza (1980) was a 1950s Ferrari/Aston Martin-inspired sports car with Cortina basis (production: 7) which was revived with Jaguar basis in 1993.
KUBELWAGEN. Accurate early 1980s Kubelwagen replica based on (what else?) the VW Beetle.
KUDOS 1992-date. Took over the Pelland (qv) Sports.
KUSTOM. Drearily familiar early 1970s beach buggy formula.
KVA 1982-date. Originators of the Ford GT 40 replica trade, with Ford's blessing. Both MkI and, uniquely, MkIII body styles. Most other replicas derived from KVA, which lost out by being difficult to build. Complete kits marketed by Madison (qv) from 1992.
KYOTE 1971-74/1976. Good-looking and practical buggy with doors and estate rear. GP (qv) bought the moulds. Production: 28. Recently revived by GT Mouldings (qv).

L

LAKES. See Voyager.
LALANDE 1983-85. Revival of GP's (qv) Centron Mk2. Production: 2. Passed on to MDB (qv).
LAMBERT 1970-72. Makers of the Opus (qv), also offered a Mini-Moke replica kit.
LATHAM 1983-date. Triumph Dolomite-based sports car, the F2 Super Sports, with hugely long gestation period.
LEA-FRANCIS 1937-53/1960/ 1980-date. Fine-handling sports cars. Postwar models: 12HP/14HP/14/70/ 18HP/2.5-litre. Total production: 3,595. Abortive Lynx sports car of 1960 was a fiasco of styling. Revival of 1980 was a recreation of pre-war Lea-Francis style on Jaguar parts. Later hardtop Ace of Spades model was a ridiculous mixture of styles; convertible added in 1992.
LEAPING CATS 1983(?)-84(?). One of the makers of the Viking (qv) and a pricey Jaguar C-Type replica.
LE MANS SPORTS CARS. Jaguar XKSS, C- and D-Type replicas of the late 1980s.
LE MARQUIS. See RJD.
LEMAZONE 1984-87. Took on the Pulsar and SN1 from Amplas (qv), renaming the latter the Comet. Also revived the Beaujangle (qv) in 1985.
LENHAM. Famous GRP panel-maker essayed the Lenham GT in 1969, a road version of its sports-racer. Production: 2. The Lenham-Healey of 1977 was a stark GRP and aluminium roadster on an Austin-Healey chassis. Production had ground to a halt by 1982. Production: approx. 20.
LEONARD 1954. Chassis and a barchetta GRP special body — one of the first.
LEOPARD 1988-date. See Mirach.
LEOPARD CRAFT 1991-date. Bugatti-esque open two-seater on Herald chassis.
LESTER 1949-1955. MG-based sports cars with basic aluminium bodies, plus a GRP coupé.
LIBRA 1985-87(?). Made the King Cobra on Cortina bits in 427 and 289 styles.
LIGHT CAR COMPANY 1991-date. Gordon Murray's £38,000 Yamaha-engined Rocket offered 143 mph in a tiny cigar-shaped fun package.
LIGHTNING 1984-85. Unconvincing Corvette copy with Cortina parts.
LIGHTSPEED. See Magenta.
LIMITED EDITION 1983-84. Californian was a GP-like buggy.

***Above:** 1990 Leopard Mirach*

Opposite page
***Top:** 1990 Maelstrom*
***Below:** 1983 MCA Coupé*

LINDY 1991-date. Vaguely Ferrari 166-inspired sports kit, the Lindy Type 48, for Spitfire chassis.
LISTAIR 1986-90. Modified the ex-Pelland (qv) into the Listair Dash. Sold out to Dash (qv).
LISTER. Jaguar XJS souper-uppers launched a replica of the 1958 Lister-Jaguar 'Knobbly' in 1990.
LITTON. See Allora.
LLOYD 1936-1951. 650cc sports car, too heavy and expensive for much success.
LMB 1960-62. Chassis for various proprietary shells and Ford sidevalve or BMC 'B'-series engines. EB shells with LMB chassis called the Debonair.
LOMAX 1983-date. Popular range of eccentric 2CV-based kits. **(7)**
LR. See Ram.
LUNA BUG 1970-71. Blatant copy of Stimson Minibug (qv).
LYNX 1974-date. Very fine Jaguar replicas. **(6)**
LYNX 1985-86. Ford Capri-based jeep-style vehicle, the Lynx Bobtail.

M

MACHO 1988. Yes, someone really called their kit car the Macho.
MACINTOSH 1990/1992-date. Mini mid-engined open two-seater of modern design. Became the ADT Sprint.
MADISON 1990-date. The Ford-engined version of the GP (qv) Madison was sold to the Madison Sportscar Company. It also marketed the complete KVA (qv) kit from 1992.
MAELSTROM 1986/1990-date. Pig ugly basic sports car with Cortina engine but fine ASD-designed spaceframe. Revived in 1990 by PACE (qv).
MAGENTA 1972-86. Strange-looking fun cars. **(5)**
MAGNUM 1987-92. Lightweight spaceframe Cobra 427 replica. Production: 40.
MAHCON. See Hutson.
MAHDEEN 1991-date. Cheap plans-built Lotus Seven-type car.
MALIBU 1991-date. Renault 4-based open fun car.
MALLALIEU 1974-81. Bentley Mk6-based tourers. **(6)**
MALLOCK 1959-date. Low-cost racing car constructor also built two dual-purpose road-going models: the Mk6R of 1967 and the Mk10 of 1969.
MALLOCK 1991-date. Arthur Mallock's son Ray made a GRP and spaceframe GT40 replica, the RML, claimed to reach 180mph.
MANTA RAY 1969-80/1986. Semi-original beach buggy. **(5)**
MANTIS. See Dutton.
MANX 1991-date. Citroen 2CV-based sports/fun car.
MARAUDER 1950-52. Rover 75-based open and coupé sports models. Production: 15.
MARCOS 1959-71/1981-date. One of the most successful and respected specialist names. **(4)**
MARKHAM-PEASEY. Two GRP specials shells of the 1950s: the Super Sabre (for Austin Seven chassis) and the Sabre De Luxe (for Ford).
MARLBOROUGH 1985-86. Slab-sided Marina-based 'traditional' roadster.
MARLIN 1979-date. Pretty and strong-selling roadsters. **(7)**
MARTIN. Early example of the specials era bodyshell.
MARTLET 1982-date. A classic car restorer's basic sports car.
MASTERCO 1992-date. Yet another Countach copy.
MAY 1991. Chris Field-designed sports car called the ECU for which the May Corporation hoped to find a sponsor.
MAYA. See Camber.
MB 1984-86(?). Self-build open sports car for Austin Seven- or Vauxhall Viva-based chassis.

MBC. See Embeesea.
MC 1984-date. Near-copy of the Turner (qv) with 2+2 seating and Viva, Escort, Marina or Datsun 120Y engines. Assumed by Carlton (qv) in 1989.
MCA 1983-date. Small Fiat 126-based coupé. Passed through Minari (qv) and settled with Dash (qv) also as a convertible.
McCOY 1984-date. Clan Crusader lookalike but with front-mounted Mini or Metro power. Also the McIVoy estate version and, from 1992, a Sierra-based Triumph TR2 replica.
McLAREN 1964-date. One of the most successful F1 teams in the sport's history. The M6GT was a road-going version of the M6 Can-Am racer. Production: 3. In 1992 McLaren showed its prototype F1, a 'hypercar' powered by a BMW V12 engine and engineered by Gordon Murray. Production was scheduled to start in 1993.
McLEAN. See Nimbus.
MDB 1986-87. Took on the Embeesea (qv) Charger 1 (Saratoga), Charger 2 (Saturn) and GP (qv) Centron (Sapphire). The Chargers went to Viking (qv).
MERLIN 1980-date. Perhaps the prettiest traditional-style kit. **(7)**
METALINE 1981-85. One of the first Cobra replicas, with an aluminium body. Were any sold?
MFE 1984-87. The Magic was an odd-looking fun car for MGB parts and, later, Cortina bits. Passed on to Scorhill (qv).
MICROPLAS. Typical 1950s specials firm. **(2)**
MIDAS 1978-date. One of the most laudable specialist enterprises ever. **(7)**
MIDDLEBRIDGE 1988-90. Inheritors of the Reliant Scimitar GTE, updated in over 200 areas (including the 2.9-litre Granada V6). Too old and too expensive.
MIDTEC 1991-date. Noble (qv)-designed Ford Cortina mid-engined open sports/fun car. Midtec also made the Midas (qv) Bronze from 1992.
MILANO. See S&J.
MINARI 1990-date. Clean-looking Alfasud-based two-seat sports car.
MINI CUB. See Andersen.
MINIJEM 1966-76. One of two projects born of the DART prototype; the other was the Mini-Marcos (qv). Passed through several firms, including one which made the Futura (qv). Production: 350. The Kingfisher Sprint (qv) was based on a Minijem shell.
MINI-MARCOS. See Marcos.
MINI MOTORS. See Stimson.
MINI-SCAMP. See Scamp.
MINION 1983-87. Quite attractive trad-style kits, the fixed-head Jackal and open Sports on Viva (later Cortina) basis. Also the Jackdaw van. From 1986 known as the Imperial.
MINUS 1982-date. Ex-Status lowered GRP Mini shell and Mini-based estate kit, the Maxi, plus a 'Group B'-style lowered Mini, the 4R2.
MIRACH 1988-92. Chris Field-designed sports car which updated the Lotus Seven concept. Rover V8 four-litre power and 150mph. Production: 10.
MIRAGE 1988-date. Fairly faithful to the prevailing Countach replica norm.
MIRKO 1984. Ambitious plan for Alfasud-based open sports car.
MOKO 1984. BMC 1100-based aluminium-bodied replica of — guess what?
MONICA 1971-75. Anglo-French four-door supercar. **(6)**
MORGAN 1910-date. Purveyors of motoring nostalgia, rather too mainstream for the scope of this book. Two hiccoughs in the established pattern: The Plus Four Plus (1963-66) was a closed, modern GRP sports car and hence anathema to Morgan fans. Production: 26. And the SLR Morgan (1963-65) was a beautiful Chris Lawrence aluminium-bodied coupé. Production: 3.
MOSQUITO. Small Mini-based doorless three-wheeler of the 1970s. Production: 6. Revived as the Triad (qv).
MOSQUITO 1989-date. Sand rail-type kit with Mini engine mounted amidships.
MOSS 1981-date. Popular kit roadsters. **(7)**
MOTORVILLE 1987-date. Revived and modified version of the Fairthorpe (qv) made in the old Fairthorpe factory.
MR. See Pulsar.
MUMFORD 1971-date. Hilarious rat-like three-wheeler on Viva components. Same manufacturer in intermittent production for over 20 years! Mumford also marketed the Lomax (qv) in the mid-1980s.
MVM 1956. Guernsey's only motor car: a small open sports car with a 325cc Anzani engine. Never fully productionised.

NACO. Unprepossessing saloon and estate bodyshells of the 1950s.
NAVAJO 1984-86. Well-engineered BMC 100-based steel jeep kit.
NAYLOR 1985-86. Fully-built MG TF replica. **(8)**
NCF 1985-date. The Diamond was a large metal-bodied estate kit, also available with a soft top.
NELSON 1989-date. Powerful and originally styled sports car using Rover V8 power, dubbed the S530.
NG 1979-89. Wide range of classically styled kits. **(7)**
NICKRI. Four GRP specials: the open Spyder and Challenger, plus the coupé Alpine and Champion.
NIFTY 1984. Abortive Mini-based GRP estate kit.
NIMBUS 1984-87. Promising mid-engined coupé using Mini/Metro power. Convertible version didn't help poor sales.
NIMROD 1973/1979/1981-86. Crazy Mini-based fun-wagon, revived by Nova (qv), then TACCO. Production: 20.
NOBLE 1985-date. Lee Noble's operation began with the Ultima and went on to encompass the Ultima Mk2 and Mk3, the P4 Ferrari replica, 23 (Lotus 23 replica) and the Midtec (qv). Also imported a US-made Porsche Spyder replica. **(7)**
NOMAD. See Foers.
NORDEC 1949. Supercharged Ford 10-powered sports car.
NOTA 1972. Australian Mini-based sports car similar to Status Minipower (qv), called the Nota Fang.
NOVA 1971-date. The glassfibre-shell-on-a-Beetle which started a kit revolution. **(5)**
NYMPH. See Bohanna Stables.
NYVREM 1986. 'Nirvana' means 'place of spiritual bliss' — as far removed as possible from this execrable Cortina-based two-seat kit of the same name.

OASIS 1990-92. The Scorpion was a revival of the Citroen Mehari corrugated jeep for 2CV chassis. Taken over by Scorhill (qv).
O&C 1984-88. Competition-orientated kits with a choice of Escort, Morris Minor and Toyota Celica engines. Models: Sport/Sprint/ Super Sport/Thruxton/Sonnet/ Serac SS.
OGLE 1960-date. Various low-production projects. **(4)**
ONE-SIX-TWO 1983-86. Marketed, then made, the Swiss Albar range of buggies, the Jet sports coupé and the bizarre six-headlamp Sonic, all Beetle-based.
OPPERMAN 1956-59. Laurie Bond-designed Unicar was a crude 328cc GRP microcar, also available in kit form. Production: 200. The fine-looking Stirling 2+2 coupé never got into its stride. Production: 2.
OPUS 1966-72. Quite horrid fun hot rod. **(3)**
OSWALD 1991-date. Body/chassis kit Frazer Nash Le Mans Replica replica for Bristol parts.
OTTERCRAFT. See Steadman.
OWEN 1973/1978/1983. Jaguar-based 'also ran' sports four-seater. **(6)**

PACE 1990-92. Lancia Beta-based Quadriga was a Ferrari 328 lookalike. PACE also took over the Maelstrom (qv).
PANACHE 1982-87. Revolting Countach 'lookalike' for VW chassis or mid-mounted Rover V8, plus the LP400 Countach 'replica'. Absolutely no panache.
PANTHER 1972-date. Golden child of the specialist marques of the 1970s. **(6,8)**
PARABUG 1971-78. Symmetrically square VW-based jeep thingy.
PARAMOUNT 1949-56. Good-looking sports open two-seater with rather anaemic Ford 10 power (later Ford Consul) and aluminium-on-ash body. Production: 72.
PARIS. See Merlin.
PASTICHE 1989-90. Took over the entire NG (qv) range, plus the Midas (qv). After a troubled existence, the rights were bought by GTM (qv).
PEEL 1955-66. Odd range of kits and microcars from Manx firm. **(4)**
PEERHOUSE. Early 1980s off-shoot of Sandwood (qv), making the Alto, a close copy of the Avante (qv). Revived briefly in 1988 by Cardo Engineering.

Right: *1986 O&C Sprint*

Opposite page
Mosquito

PEERLESS 1957-60. TR3-based grand tourer **(2)**. Re-emerged as the Warwick (qv).
PELLAND 1979-92. Ex-Falcon (qv) man Peter Pellandine's return. **(5)**
PENNON. Bugatti Type 35 replica of the mid-1980s.
PEREGRINE 1961. Falcon (qv) body on Terrier (qv) chassis.
PERRY. See AD.
PETERSEN 1992-date. Bentley Speed Six replica.
PHOENIX 1983-86. Ex-Clan (qv) man Paul Haussauer made this GRP monocoque Mini estate.
PHOENIX. See Sylva.
PIKE 1986-88. Ford-based Morgan-esque kit roadster, first known as the Invader, then the Predator.
PILGRIM 1984-date. Successful budget kit manufacturer. **(7)**
PIMLICO. See Domino.
PIPER 1967-74. Attractive enthusiasts' sports cars. **(5)**
PKA. A Jaguar V12-engined Daytona Spyder replica of the late 1980s.
POWERBUG 1970-71. Copy of the Vulture (qv) beach buggy.
POWERDRIVE 1955-57. Alloy-bodied 322cc open three-wheeler.
PROBE 1969-72. Dennis Adams' design series. **(6)**
PROTEUS. See Deltayn.
PROTEUS. See Copycats.
PROVA 1986-date. Replicas of Lamborghinis Countach and Miura, with Renault V6 or Rover 16V power.
PSR. See Minus.
PULSAR 1978-82. Concept (qv) Centaur Mk2 2+2 and Mk3 back in business as the Pulsar 2 and 3. Taken over by MR Developments in 1980.
PULSAR. See Amplas.
PYTHON 1979-date. One of the UK's first, and best, 427 Cobra replicas.

Q

QUANTUM 1988-date. Fiesta-based four-seat monocoque coupé.
QUASAR UNIPOWER 1968. Insane glass cube. **(9)**
QUEST 1969-70. Genuine attempt to market the *UFO* car. **(9)**

***Above:** 1987 Prova*
***Left:** 1988 Quantum*

R

RACECORP 1990-date. LA Roadster was Lotus 7-style sportster with Ford power.
RAFFO 1985-date. Alfa Romeo mid-engined road/race sports car.
RAILTON 1989-date. Jaguar XJ-S-based revival of a famous marque, by William Towns.
RAM 1984-date. Sports replica specialists, duplicating the AC Cobra (SC), D-Type (LM), XKSS (SS) and Ferrari Daytona Spyder (RT), all with Alan Reynard spaceframes.
RAM. See Regis.
RANGER 1971-76/1984-85. Successful Moke-type kit, plus a Mini-based three-wheeler. **(5)**
RAPPORT 1980-82. Another Chris Humberstone enterprise. **(8)**
RAT. See FF.
RAWLSON 1971-date. Race-car firm offered the Group 5 CR8 of 1972 in road guise with Renault or Simca parts. In 1976 it built a one-off 250LM replica which was productionised in 1982 with Beetle power, then Alfasud. Marketed by Replicar (qv), then Sharman, it never got the push it needed, so was sold on to Classic Replicars, later Western Classics (qv).
REEVES 1988-91. Mid-engined coupé kit which never reached production.
REFLEX 1987-date. Mid-engined coupé for Lancia Beta or Ford Escort engines.
REGIS 1985/1989-date. Cortina-based coupé kit. **(7)**
REJO 1961-62. Pretty GRP body on spaceframe chassis with Ford Pop power.
RENEGADE 1970-74. American-designed beach buggy. Production: 200. Also Dutch-designed Renegade T buggy/hot rod. GP (qv) bought all the moulds and offered buggies until 1976.
REPLICAR 1981-date. Persistent fringe member of the kit scene with the Beetle-based Type 35 (latterly made by PBM, then Lurastore), Type 43 four-seater and imports of a Jaguar SS100 replica; then marketed Rawlson's (qv) Ferrari 250LM replica; then the Cursor microcar **(8)**; and lastly a Sherpa van-based Bugatti 55 replica.
REVOLUTION. Rear-engined trike of the 1970s.
RGS 1947-60(?). Revival of the JAG (qv) in 1954 plus the first GRP shells sold in Britain, in open and fastback styles.
RHINO 1981-83. VW-based jeep taken over by Eagle (qv).
RICKMAN 1987-date. Highly successful kit maker. **(7)**
RJD 1980-date. After Panther (qv), Robert Jankel instigated the Le Marquis brand-name and made various exotic limousines and drop-head conversions. The Gold Label of 1987 was a Bentley Turbo R-powered open two-seater costing £250,000; just two per year were made.

Above: *1988 RJD Gold Label*
Left: *1991 Royale*

Opposite page
1984 Scorpion

The Corvette ZR1-based Tempest (1990) was a supercharged beast claimed to be the fastest open car made, at 205mph.
RLT 1991-date. Ex-Moss (qv) John Cowperthwaite back with an Escort-based DIY jeep called the Husky.
RMB 1973-date. Long-running MG TF replica called the Gentry on Herald chassis — later with Ford-based option. Also an abortive replica called the Heeley. Project passed to SP motors in 1989.
RML. See Mallock.
ROBERTSON. Bentley Mk6-based tourer of the early 1980s.
ROBIN HOOD 1984-date. Ferrari Daytona Spyder replica on chopped Rover SD1, then with a Jaguar V12-based chassis, then as a conversion of a Triumph TR7. Ferrari objected to them all, so reverted to making the S7, a Lotus Seven lookalike, from 1989, plus the S6.
ROBLEY. See Sylva.
ROCA 1988. American-designed Porsche 911 replica with chassis to accommodate front-, mid- and rear-mounted Ford engines!
ROCHDALE 1952-68. One of the most popular early specialists. **(3)**
ROCKET. See Light Car Company.
RONART 1986-date. Fabulously stark Jaguar-powered sports car. **(7)**
ROSE 1967-date. One of the first Bentley Mk6 roadster shells, styled by Neville Trickett.
ROTRAX. See Adams.
ROYALE 1991-date. Open five-seater 'traditional tourer kit.
RS. Early 1990s Jaguar C-Type replica.
RUGGER 1980-81. US-designed all-steel jeep replica on VW Beetle chassis.
RW 1983-date. Took on the Karma from AD (qv), offering both rear -engined Beetle and Ford front- and mid-engined versions. Also a VW-engined trike and Cobra 427.
RYDER 1981-82. Took over the Pelland (qv), also offered a VW-based Morgan replica, called the Rembrandt and Royale. Made by Graham Autos from 1982 to 1984, then briefly by Sabre (qv). The Pelland went to Listair (qv).

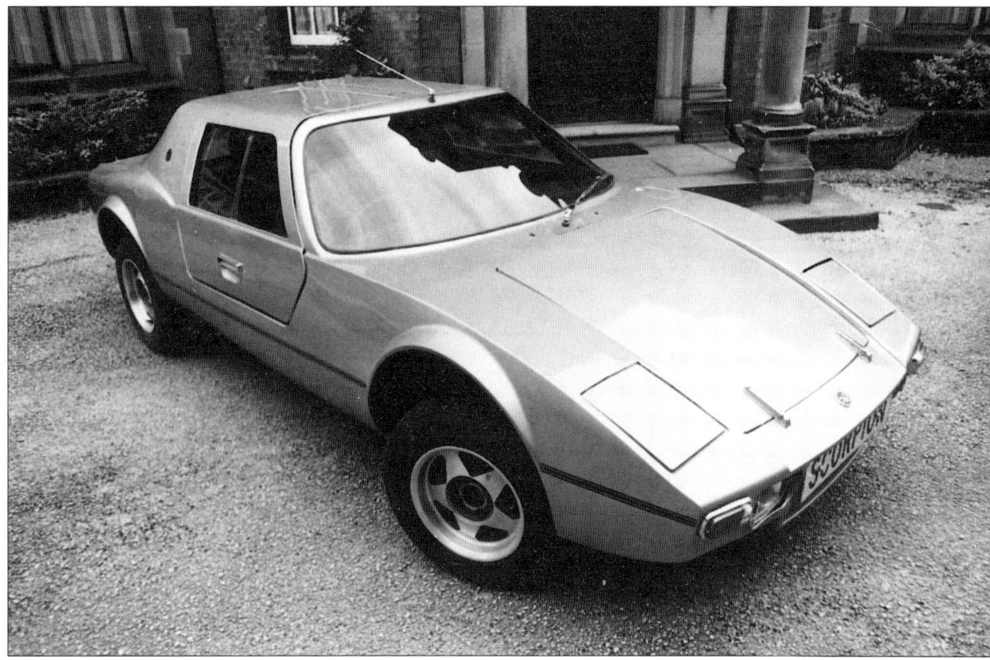

S 

SABRE 1984-86. Crude Mini-based four-seat hatchback called the Sprint. Later an open version, the Vario. Briefly took on the Ryder (qv) cars.
SAFIR 1981-date. 'Genuine' Ford GT40 replica. **(8)**
SAGESSE 1990-91. Ambitious Ford CVH mid-engined 2+2 coupé called the Helios. Production: 3.
SANDBACH 1983-84. Imported, then made, a VW Beetle-based MG TD replica.
S&J 1984-86. Lovely four-seater GRP convertible on Alfa GTV basis called the Milano, plus the stillborn Sportiva.
S&R. See Embeesea Eurocco. **(7)**
SANDWOOD 1983-84. Made the Alfachassis, an Alfasud-engined replacement for Beetle chassis. Developed replicas of the Porsche Speedster, AC Cobra and Jaguar XK120, marketed DJ's (qv) Mongoose and launched the Gopher sand-rail. Just after changing its name to Classic Reproductions, it was taken over by Sheldonhurst (qv).
SARRONSET. See Stimson.
SCAMP 1970-date. Most popular of all the Moke-style kits. **(5)**
SCARAB 1972. Ugly Mini mid-engined sports coupé.
SCHUPPAN 1992-date. Builders of the Porsche 962CR sports-racer developed a version for the road: £770,000-worth of 217mph road-crusher.
SCORHILL 1987-date. Took on the MFE (qv) Magic. In 1992 relaunched the Oasis (qv) as the El Cid, in kit form; then the Dutton (qv) Melos and Legerra.
SCORPION 1972-75/1984-85. Designed by Killeen (qv), this Imp-engined gullwing coupé was ambitious, but a bad economy and poor management killed it. Production: 11. Revived in 1984 with Alfasud power as the Kestrel Scorpion.
SCOTT ELLIS RACING 1989-date. GT40 replica plus the Chevron (qv) B8.
SCOTTISH REPLICARS & CLASSICS 1984. Build-to-order firm offering MG TF and Porsche replicas.
SD500 1987. Gorgeous Ferrari 500 Mondial replica with Alfa Romeo GTV engine. Later made by Transformer (qv).
SEAGULL 1984. Ugly GRP and aluminium Mini-based mid-engined open two-seater.
SEASPRAY 1971. Rip-off of the Manta Ray (qv).
SEM 1989-date. TVR lookalike for Cortina bits called the Saiga.
SERAPH 1984-87. First model was

Above: *1991 Scott Ellis Racing Chevron B8 GT*

the Sports Racer, a mid-engined Ford-based spaceframe coupé which was pushed aside by the acquisition in 1985 of the ex-AED (qv) Bonito.

SETA 1976-78. Boxy VW-based gullwing coupé, later known as the Zeta.

SEVERN 1990-91. Plans-built version of — guess what?

SHADO 1990-date. The Sorrento was originally a huge Jaguar V12-powered coupé, then was redesigned with a Honda CBR 'bike engine. Production versions were to be Sierra-engined.

SHADOW. See Kingfisher Mouldings.

SHAMROCK 1955. Rather ugly sports car — one prototype only.

SHAPECRAFT. See Birchfield.

SHARK 1971-72. Mayfly of the buggy world. Production 300. Also Shark T. Production: 2.

SHARMAN. See Rawlson.

SHEEN 1964-65. Worthy Imp-based two-seat coupé grandiloquently called the Sheen Imperator GTS. Production: 2 proto- types.

SHEFFIELD BEACH BUGGY 1970. A buggy made — you guessed it — in Sheffield.

SHELDONHURST 1984-86. Acquired the Sandwood (qv) shebang of models: Cobra, Speedster, Mongoose, Gopher, XK120, and the Rawlson (qv) 250LM with the Alfachassis.

SHELSLEY 1983-84. Good-looking spaceframe chassis roadster, the Spyder, with engines from Ford up to Lotus Twin-Cam.

SHEPHERD 1985-86. Cardboard cut-out-style utility thing for Cortina parts.

SHERWOOD 1984-date. Spartan's (qv) practical stablemate. **(7)**

SHIRLEY. Dumpy GRP 1950s shell originally known as the Kenmar.

SHRIVE 1969-80(?) Early Bentley Mk6 special with GRP body and steel wings.

SIENNA 1988-date. Reasonable Countach replica.

SILHOUETTE 1970-72. Outsized GRP sports coupé body on VW chassis, from 1971 with gullwing doors and known as the Zagaroff. Production: 12.

SILHOUETTE 1987-89(?). Abysmal Countach copy called the SC5000S.

SILURIAN 1992-date. Huge 1920s-style open tourer with four doors and meticulous construction.

SINCLAIR 1985. Sir Clive's brief madness. **(9)**

SIVA 1969-76. Veritable explosion of kits from Neville Trickett. **(5,6)**

SK 1985-86. MGB-based, Allard-style roadster.

SKIP 1990-date. Mini-based three-wheeler in the AF (qv) mode.

SKORPION 1986-87. A Skoda-based coupé kit — it's true! — called the Chikara.

SLR. See Morgan.
SN1. See Lemazone.
SOUTHERN ROADCRAFT 1985-date. Two replicas: the SR V8 (Cobra) and the V12 (Daytona Spyder).
SOUTH WEST REPLICAS 1990-date. Beautiful Lotus 23 replica called the Xanthos Type 90.
SP 1972-75. Two prototypes: The SP Highwayman, a six-cylinder traditional-style roadster, and the SP2, a Rover V8-engined sports estate.
SP. See RMB.
SPARTAN 1973-date. Hugely popular MG-inspired kit. Joined in 1991 by the Fiesta-based utility Treka. **(5,7)**
SPECFRAME 1983-85. Fine chassis but dreadful styling for the Cortina-based Spectre.

Top: *1976 Seta*
Above: *1990 Shado Sorrento*

Opposite page
1985 Stallion

SPEEDEX. Jem Marsh — later of Marcos (qv) — made several specials shells: the 750 and Silverstone for Austin Sevens and the Sirocco for Fords.
SPIRIT 1984-85. Took over AD's (qv) Mercedes SSK replica for VW or Cortina components. Bought by Daytona Classics (qv).
SPM 1990-date. Ferrari 328 lookalike based on the Pontiac Fiero.
SPORTS CAR SERVICES 1985-87. Cobra replicators plus an abortive Corvette replica, the Mako.
SPYDER 1985-88. Famous Lotus chassis builder made the Silverstone, a Lotus Seven-style spaceframe sportster. Production: 40.
SQUIRE 1984-date. Beautifully-made replica of the 1930s Squire with Ford, then Alfa Romeo, engines.
STALLION 1985. 'Noddy's staff car' was one description of this Heath Robinson Jaguar-based four-seater.
STANBURY 1983-86. Stark plans-built trials-style car for Herald chassis.
STARCRAFT. See Sherwood.
STARDUST 1990-date. Escort basis says it all for this 'D-Type lookalike'.
STATUS 1971-84/1991-date. The wonderful world of Brian Luff. **(5)**
STEADMAN. Late 1980s Jaguar XJ6-based SS100 replica with aluminium body.
STEANEY. See Embeesea.
STENGEL. Eccentric Peter Stengel removed Rolls-Royce bodies and replaced them with his own neo-classic designs during the 1980s.
STEVENS 1972-84(?). One for the lost causes file. **(6)**
STIMSON 1970-83. Whacky fun cars of genius and abandon. **(5)**
STRADA 1974-75. Brave Ford Mexico mid-engined sports coupé called the Strada 4/88. Wrong price, wrong time. Production: 2, plus 4 unbuilt cars.
STREET BEETLE. Late 1980s Porsche 356 Speedster replica dubbed the Chesil Speedster, still available.
SUMMERFIELD 1992-date. First car (1993) the Solar, a Lola Mk1 replica designed largely for competition use with spaceframe chassis and Alfa twin-cam power.
SUN. See TMC.
SUNLIT 1983-84. Italian-designed GRP coupé body for Fiat 500/126.
SUPER 1960-65. Austin Seven special bodies, the 750 and Sportsman, and the Super Two for Ford 1172 basis, of which over 200 were made.
SUTOL 1986-date. Beautiful Lotus 23 replica.
SVC. See Specframe.
SWALLOW DORETTI 1954-55. Fine TR2-based sports car. **(2)**
SWIFT 1983-85(?). Well-built but failed 'trad' sports car. **(8)**
SWIFT CLASSICS 1988. V12-powered Ferrari Daytona replica.
SWINDON SPORTS CARS. See Vincent & Sylva.
SYD LAWRENCE 1972-79(?). Excellent Bentley Mk6-based specials.
SYLVA 1982-date. Respected range of road/race sports cars. **(7)**

Above: *1987 Transformer HF2000*
Left: *1963 Triton*

T

TA. See NG.
TA 1989-date. Odd-looking door-less fun car, the Spirit, for Escort/Cortina parts; also the Phantom, an open two-seater based on an Ashley (qv) shell.
TAG. See UVA.
T&A. The Predator, a Jaguar-based Cobra copy of the early 1990s.
T&J 1989-date. Took on the JC (qv) Midge and Locust and added the Cortina-based Hornet.
TALON 1988-date. Took on the GP (qv) Talon, adding a mid-mounted Ford Fiesta-based chassis and a full convertible body.
TEAL 1984-date. Renowned Bugatti replicators. **(7)**
TECHNIC 1987-date. Beetle-based replica of the Porsche 550 Spyder.
TEMPEST 1988-date. Small Reliant Fox-based 'trad' roadster.
TERRIER 1959-61. Len Terry-designed Ford Pop-based sports car.
THOROUGHBRED. See Merlin.
TI 1985-86. A Cobra replica called the Tuscan.
TICI 1972-73. Diminutive city fun car. **(5)**
TIGER 1991-date. The Super 6, a Lotus Seven-style car, and the ex-Western Classics (qv) 250LM, re-engineered for VW Golf power.
TIGRESS 1983-85. Scottish Beetle-based 'exotic'.
TKH. See Venom.
TMC 1983-84/1987-88/1990-91(?). The Scout was a Moke-style car, later made by AEM, then Sun.
TOJEIRO 1952-54. AC Ace designer's own sports chassis.
TORNADO 1958-63. Successful minor sports car manufacturer. **(2)**
TORNADO 1987-date. Beetle-based or mid-engined McLaren M6 replica; Ford GT40 copy; and a six-wheeled motorhome called the Continental.
TOWNEND. Obscure 1950s special.
TRAC 1991-date. Faithful Jaguar SS100 replica.
TRAKKA 1984. Renault 4-based utility.
TRAMP 1970-71. Richard Oakes' first design, an original buggy. Production: 75.
TRANSFORMER 1986-date. Highly successful replica of the Lancia Stratos, the HF2000, using mid-mounted Lancia engine and later Honda, Alfa Romeo and even Ferrari engines. Also took on the SD500 (qv). The HF2000 was also offered by Hawkridge Developments (qv). Also a Dino replica.
TRIAD 1992-date. Revival of the Mosquito (qv) three-wheeler.
TRIDENT 1967-74/1976-77. Pretty sports coupé which almost made it. **(4)**
TRIDENT AUTOVET 1984-85. Also known as Ferrante, took over the AD (qv) 400, renaming it Chimera.
TRIKING 1979-date. Superb evocation of Morgan Super Sports. **(8)**
TRIPLE C 1985-date. Maker of the Challenger. **(7)**
TRIPPER. See TX.
TRIPOS 1984-90. Barrel-bodied sports car with Ford engines which showed promise but never really got going. Also imported the Hunter roadster from the USA.
TRITON 1963. Racer for the road with claimed 140mph from BMC 'B'-series engine. Production: 2.
TROLL 1986-date. Well-made trials-type car and, later, a Lotus Seven-style sports car.
TURNER 1951-66. Popular sports car maker. **(2)**
TVR 1953-date. Famous and now highly successful specialist. Fringe projects included the Trident (qv), the Tina **(4)**, the SM sports estate of 1971 and the 420 Sports Saloon of 1985.
TWM. 1950s Ford/BMC-based chassis and GRP bodies.
TX 1971-79/1983-84/1986. Wibbly-wobbly fun car. **(5)**

UFO 1970-71. Outer space range of psychedelic buggies.
UNICORN 1987. Lotus Seven-style kit.
UNIPOWER 1966-70. Highly-regarded Mini mid-engined sports car. **(3)**
UNIQUE AUTOCRAFT. See Python.
UVA 1981-date. Kit manufacturer renowned for quality and commitment to the cause. **(7)**

VANCLEE 1983-date. 2CV-based jeepie of Belgian origin, later made by Dutton (qv), then JPR (qv).
VANWALL 1990-date. Revival of the 1950s F1 marque with mid-engined V8 supercar, still awaited.
VEGANTUNE. See Evante.
VENOM 1985-87. Early, and dreadful, Countach replica.
VERSIL. Little-known GRP special of the 1950s.
VIKING 1980-83. Jaguar-based aluminium-bodied SS100-style roadster. Co-designers split, so was also made contemporaneously by Leaping Cats (qv).
VIKING 1987. Last refuge of the Embeesea (qv) Chargers, now called the Dragonfire and Dragonfly.
VIKING MINISPORT. See Peel.
VINCENT 1982-date. Two models: the Hurricane, a 1960s-style open two-seater; and the Brooklands and MPH (replicas of the Riley MPH). The former went to Domino (qv), the latter to Swindon Sports Cars, then Dwornik.
VINDICATOR 1989-date. Basic Sierra-based two-seater sports kit.
VISCOUNT 1985-86. Copy of the Burlington (qv) Arrow.
VIXEN. Rare 1950s special.
VOLKSROD 1968-date. The UK's first-ever buggy. **(5)**
VOODOO 1971-73. Quite possibly the greatest 'lost cause' kit car of all. **(5)**
VOYAGER 1984-85. Crude roadster based on Beetle, then Viva, parts.
VULTURE 1970-72. Scavenger of GP Buggy shell. Production: 130.
VW 1961. No relation — a pretty fastback coupé.

Above: *1980 Viking*
Below: *1985 Voyager*

Above: 1992 Yamaha OX99-11 by Ypsilon

W

WARWICK 1960-61. Modified revival of the Peerless (qv).
WATFORD 1959-62. Chassis and shell manufacturer. **(2)**
WATLING. 1950s maker of chassis and a sports estate shell.
WESTERN CLASSICS. Took on the Rawlson (qv) 250LM in mid-engined Ford CVH-powered guise, dubbed the 164LM in 1987. Passed to Tiger (qv).
WESTFIELD 1983-date. Kit phenomenon of the 1980s. **(7)**
WESTMINSTER 1968(?)-70. Neville Trickett-designed Bentley Mk6 four-seat body shell.
WHITBY 1983-86(?). Aluminium-bodied Moke-type kit called the Warrior.
WHITTET. 1950s specials manufacturer.
WMC 1990-date. Bond Bug (qv) revived in three- and four-wheeled forms.
WSM 1962-67. New bodies for British classics. **(4)**
WYNES. See McCoy.
WYVERN 1983-86. Well-made Viva-based roadster, later with Escort power option. Latterly known as the Hawk.

XANTHOS. See South West Replicas.

YAK. See Grantura.
YAK 1979. Third world Escort-based utility jeep project called the Yak Yeoman.
YIMKIN 1958. Basic cycle-winged sports car. Production: 6.
YORK. Early 1980s Cobra replica.
YPSILON 1992-date. Makers of the Yamaha OX99-11 tandem-seat supercar, to be launched in 1994.

ZAGAROFF. See Silhouette.
ZETA. See Seta.
ZIGCLAIR 1981. MGB-engined Riley-style prototype that almost went into production.
ZITA 1971-72. Sleek VW-engined two-seater coupé. Production: 2.

Right: *HRG made a fair number of traditional sports cars with Singer engines before essaying the Twin Cam in 1955 with more modern bodywork. Although the Twin Cam was its last production model (four were made), there were some later prototypes and specials, such as this example.*
Below: *Gordon-Keeble is a name which today commands enthusiasm and respect. In its time, it attempted to rival luxury makers such as Jensen and Aston Martin, but it was simply uneconomic to manufacture and production did not exceed one hundred.*
Bottom: *Rear-mounted Imp Sport power gave Ginetta's most successful model, the G15, a keen edge. It was popular as a competition car as well as an agile and economical sports car.*

Above: *The Unipower GT measured only 40 inches high and used a Mini front subframe reversed to provide mid-engined power. Although the interior was cramped and awkward, the Unipower offered amazing handling and performance.*

Left: *GP was one of the first British beach buggy manufacturers and quickly became one of the most popular during the great buggy boom of 1970-72. There were short and long wheelbase models, estates and pick-ups. Thousands were bought, and GP still sells large numbers of these 'bathtubs' today.*

Below: *When Reliant took over Bond in 1969, Ogle's Tom Karen was able to persuade it to develop a fun three-wheeler. The Bug of 1970 was the result, a uniformly tangerine triangular projectile with a hingeing canopy and 700cc Regal engine. From 1970 to 1974, 2,562 were made.*

Above: *Two glassfibre shells for Beetle floorpans: the 1971 Nova (rear) and the 1983 RW Karma. The Nova was styled by Richard Oakes and remains one of the all-time great kit car designs. The Karma was a cruder Ferrari Dino lookalike.*

Right: *This is the prototype Stimson Mini Bug, concocted during 1970 by inventor and artist extraordinaire Barrie Stimson. Built on a budget of £25, it was the world's first Mini-based buggy and was, in the words of a sales agent, 'one of the ugliest cars around'.*

Below: *The RMB Gentry was a pretty interpretation of the MG TF, offered in kit form from 1973. Using a Triumph Herald/Vitesse chassis, it became one of the most popular kits of the 1970s and, indeed, the 1980s.*

Above: *The lovely Piper series was characterised by the excellent engineering of all models. Most used Ford engines mounted at the front and were fine handling machines. Like many kit cars, the Piper was a victim of tax changes and the oil crisis.*

Left: *Harold Dermott's Midas was a car fundamentally right in concept. The Midas Gold Convertible of 1989 was the final and most attractive development: with MG Metro power, it added incisive performance and wind-in-the-hair exhilaration to the dynamically superb Midas coupé.*

Below: *Dutton's highly successful range of kit roadsters in the 1980s included the Melos, Phaeton and B Plus S2, a revival of its basic 1970s sports car. Thousands of people were attracted by the extremely competitive pricing of the Duttons, although quality was often lacking.*

Right: *Ginetta moved away from the pure sports car theme during the 1980s. With the 1984 G26, it succeeded in offering a credible four-seater coupé in kit form, on Ford Cortina parts. Unusually for a kit car, it compared favourably with mass-produced coupés.*
Below, right: *For most people, the Dax Tojeiro was the AC Cobra replica in the UK. The best-developed and best-selling of a whole clutch of replicas, in its most fiery form it could be specified with a space-frame chassis and Jaguar V12 power.*
Bottom, right: *The thunderous Ronart evoked the lines of GP racers of the 1950s in a beautifully conceived package. A Spyder chassis gave it integrity, Jaguar power gave it phenomenal performance, and its long, low body was available in GRP or metal.*
Below: *Of dozens of replicas offered in kit form during the 1980s, perhaps the most inspired was GP's Spyder which duplicated the undoubted charm of the Porsche 718 RSK. Available with head fairings for left- or right-hand drive, it scored huge export success.*

ULTIMA
F28 LJR

Opposite page
Top right, insert: *Lee Noble's Ultima series was an excellently executed mid-engined sports car and one of the few successful attempts to create an original kit-form supercar. The curvaceous Mk3 of 1987, pictured, was easily the best.*
Main photo: *William Towns was no stranger to rebodying Jaguars; he made the E-Type-based Guyson in 1974. The Railton of 1989 was based on the Jaguar XJ-S and was available in two forms: the bespatted F29 Claremont and the more sporting F28 Fairmile. Neither proved particularly popular.*
Bottom: *Tom Walkinshaw's TWR made a name for itself as the performance and racing expedient of Jaguar. In a joint venture, TWR created the Jaguar XJR-15, a road-going 'hypercar' capable of massive performance. The 50 examples made could be raced by owners in an exclusive championship, the prize for which was $1 million.*

This Page
Top: *Incredibly, this Peel Trident was not the Manx firm's smallest model; that accolade went to the 53in long P50. The whole front section of the Trident's bodywork lifted forwards for entry into the two-seater which was, by all reports, a frightening experience to drive.*
Right: *Distinctive among the 'specials' bodyshells of the late 1950s and early 1960s was the Falcon Competition with its twin head fairings. In 1960 a basic bodyshell would have set you back all of £65.*
Bottom, right: *When the Marcos 1800 was first shown in 1964, there was nothing quite as dramatically styled or as adventurously engineered. The wooden-chassis Marcos used a large variety of Ford, Volvo and Triumph engines before its demise in 1971.*

Above: *Dennis Adams' Probe 16 of 1969 was so low off the ground — just 34in high — that passengers had to enter through a glass roof which slid back electronically. Despite the clamour of its reception, only three were officially produced.*

Left: *Way-out, whacky or just plain gruesome, the TX Tripper, designed by Torix Bennett of Fairthorpe, was certainly distinctive. Its psychedelic high-day was the fun car boom of the early 1970s, but somehow it managed to linger on in production until the end of the decade.*

Left: *The Clan Crusader was both brave and advanced, using an all-glassfibre monocoque allied to a Sunbeam Stiletto engine. It may have had an odd shape, but it sold strongly to enthusiasts who appreciated its fine handling and excellent performance.*

Opposite page
Panther Westwinds could never be accused of understatement. With the 6, they claimed to have the world's first six-wheeled 200mph car, but the prototype never ran as well as hoped. The 8.2-litre Cadillac twin-turbo engine was claimed to develop 600bhp.

XPE 384S
XPE 384S

Left: *The Marlin, produced in Cornwall from 1979, was one of the best engineered and prettiest of the many kit-form roadsters of the period. Although it used the humble Morris Marina's mechanical components, it was a car which felt 'right' from the start and was justifiably popular.*

Above: *Caterham Car Sales successfully maintained production of the Lotus Seven, improving it continually from 1973. Graham Nearn, who masterminded the model's dramatic ascendancy in the 1980s, is pictured here launching a new basic kit version in 1985.*

Left: *There were few more pure fun cars than the Kougar Sports, launched in 1977. Its spartan doorless body, reminiscent of Frazer Nash, clothed Jaguar components. There were precious few concessions to comfort or practicality.*

***Right:** The GTM is one of the great survivors of the specialist industry. The basic profile of the GTM (rear) remained unchanged in over 26 years to date. In 1985 it was joined by the convertible 2+2 GTM Rossa (foregound), which retained the GTM's mid-mounted Mini engine.*

***Below:** The name Lynx became associated with superlative Jaguar D-Type replicas in the 1970s, but it was not until 1991 that Lynx introduced its replica of Jaguar's roadgoing D-Type, the XKSS. Gloriously reproduced, the Lynx was priced at around £90,000, reflecting its hand-built nature.*

***Bottom:** McLaren's M6 was never truly marketed as a road car. In the USA a firm called Manta Cars produced a replica, the Montage, which UVA brought to Britain. UVA's own improved mid-engined version was known as the M6 GTR, after the McLaren from which it took its inspiration.*

Left: *This pretty mid-engined targa coupé from Harrier Racing is scheduled for production in 1993. Called the LR9, it uses a tuned Alfa Romeo 164 three-litre V6 engine and is claimed to reach 60mph from rest in five seconds.*

Above: *Jaguar's aborted Le Mans hopeful of 1966, the XJ13, remained a one-off. So Proteus' replica of the car, dubbed the P90, was greeted with open arms when it appeared in 1992. Stunningly accurate in every respect, it used a mid-mounted Jaguar XJ-S engine.*

Below: *The Asquith Motor Carriage Co was one of several firms offering vintage-style vans during the 1980s. In 1991 it also showed a Taxi and a Luxury Limousine, which entered production in 1992. The Limousine, shown here, could be ordered with such extras as leather trim, air-conditioning and a cocktail cabinet.*

Above: *Aston Martin stylist William Towns made several hundred of his Hustler 'modular' cars. The grandest of these was the Highlander, a six-wheeled luxury express using a Jaguar XJ12 engine. It retained the Hustler family traits of external chassis rails and sliding glass doors.*
Right: *There could hardly be a more beautiful car to replicate than Ferrari's P4 racer, whose Pininfarina body was one of the all-time greats. Lee Noble successfully produced a stunning replica, which he called the Noble P4. It was later taken over by Deon Cars.*
Below: *A rather curious profile distinguished the Gold Cirrus, the 1991 creation of ex-custom wizard Nick Butler. Its specification included four-wheel drive and a mid-mounted Rover V8 engine, and the two-seater was claimed to exceed 140mph.*

D.M.S. KIT CARS

"The Best Value for Money Kit"
You Can Buy!

CORTINA BASE £1500
SIERRA BASE £1700
JAGUAR BASE £2400
CHASSIS STARTER KITS AVAILABLE

A FANTASTIC BODY CONVERSION KIT FOR THE CAPRI
EASY FIRST TIME BUILD
GOOD INSURANCE

A STUNNING BODY CONVERSION KIT FOR THE DATSUN 240/260Z
GOOD FIRST TIME BUILD
PRACTICAL EVERY DAY USE

PHONE 0425 656476

For More Details

The KUDOS Roadster

CHOPPED BUT NOT CHANGED

- GRP MONOCOQUE CONSTRUCTION
- MID-ENGINE, ALFA BASED
- JUST 'PHONE FOR A BROCHURE

KUDOS

Based on a concept by Peter Pellandine

SQUARE ONE DEVELOPMENT, RINK DRIVE, SWADLINCOTE, DERBYSHIRE DE11 8JL
ENQUIRIES (0283) 552448 WORKSHOP (0283) 551598 FAX (0283) 552114

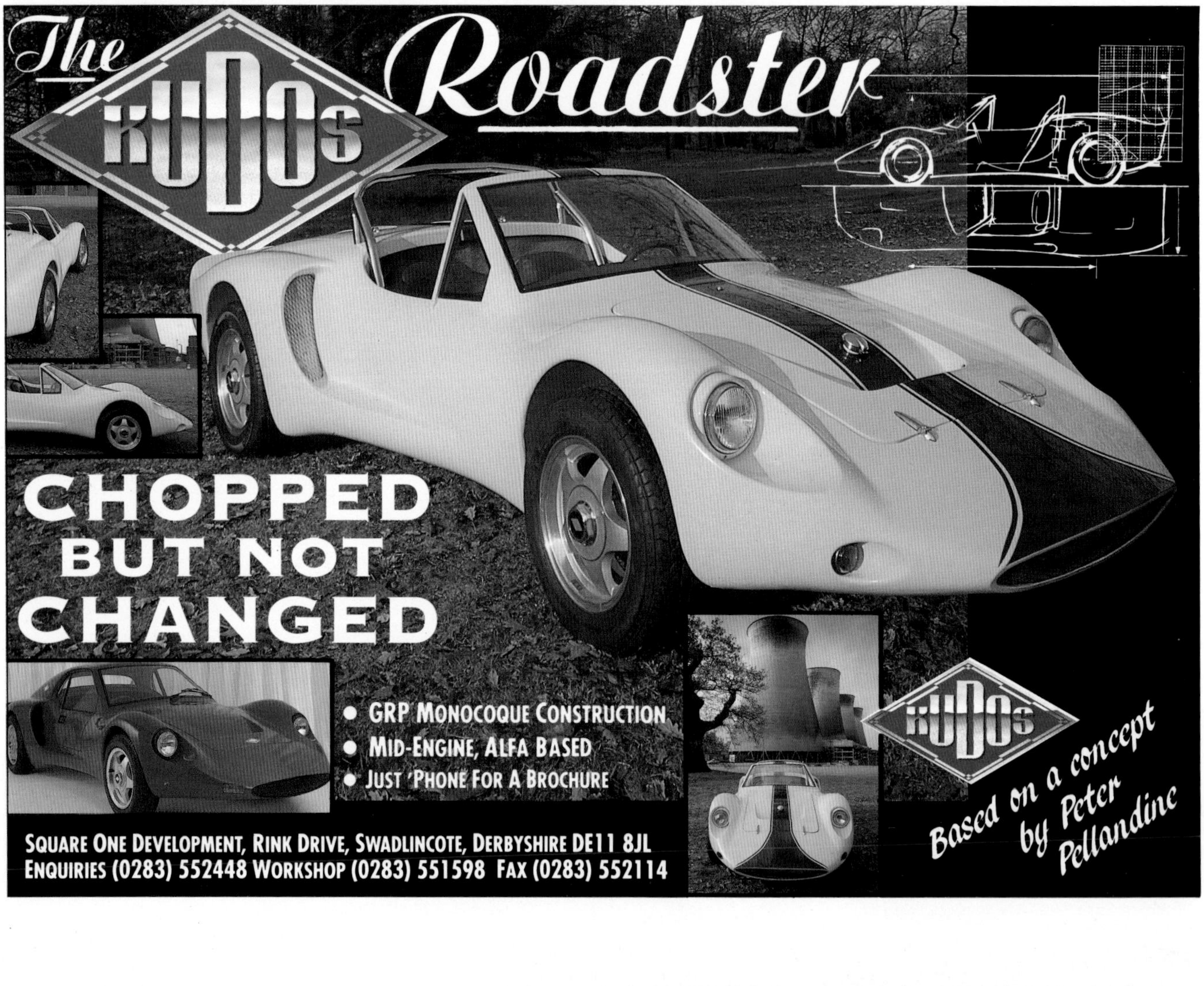